HISTORICAL ACTU
THE SOCIALIST O

Alternative to Parlia.

István Mészásros

By the same author

Satire and Reality (Szépirodalmi Könyvkiadó Budapest 1955);
La rivolta degli intellettuali in Ungheria (Einaudi 1958);
Attila József e l'arte moderna (Lerici 1964);
Marx's Theory of Alienation (Merlin Press 1970);
The Necessity of Social Control (Merlin Press 1971);
Aspects of History and Class Consciousness [ed] (Routledge 1971);
Lukács's Concept of Dialectic (Merlin Press 1972);
*Neocolonial Identity and Counter-Consciousness: The Work of
Renato Constantino* [ed] (Merlin Press 1978);
The Work of Sartre: Search for Freedom
(Harvester Wheatsheaf 1979);
Philosophy, Ideology and Social Science
(Harvester Wheatsheaf 1986);
The Power of Ideology (Harvester Wheatsheaf 1989);
Beyond Capital: Toward a Theory of Transition
(Merlin Press 1995);
L'alternativa alla società del capitale: Socialismo o barbarie
(Punto Rosso 2000);
*Socialism or Barbarism: From the "American Century" to the
Crossroads* (Monthly Review Press 2001);
A educação para além do capital (Boitempo Editorial 2005);
O desafio e o fardo do tempo histórico (Boitempo Editorial 2007);
The Challenge and Burden of Historical Time
(Monthly Review Press 2008);
The Structural Crisis of Capital (Monthly Review Press 2009);
*Estrutura social e formas de consciência: A determinação social
do método* (Boitempo Editorial 2009).

HISTORICAL ACTUALITY OF THE SOCIALIST OFFENSIVE

Alternative to Parliamentarism

István Mészáros

Professor Emeritus of Philosophy
University of Sussex

Bookmarks Publications

Historical Actuality of the Socialist Offensive
Alternative to Parliamentarism
Copyright István Mészáros
Introduction first published 2010
Chapters 1-4 excerpted from *Beyond Capital* (1995)

ISBN 978 1905 192 618

Published by Bookmarks Publications
c/o 1 Bloomsbury Street, London WC1B 3QE
Designed by Bookmarks Publications
Printed by Melita Press

CONTENTS

To the memory of
General Vasco Gonçalves
(1922-2005)
deeply committed radical socialist
Prime Minister of the Portuguese
Revolutionary Government

ALTERNATIVE TO PARLIAMENTARISM

I.

IN 1995, two years before the formation of Tony Blair's Government in Britain, I was writing in sharply negative terms about *"the coming Pyrrhic electoral victory"* of "New Labour". My concern in anticipating a social and political disaster to come after the self-deceiving electoral "victory" was not simply the state of the British Labour party. Rather, it was the much broader significance of the political developments which we had to witness for a long time, resulting in very similar retrograde transformations not only in Britain but in the Western labour movement in general. I argued that "as things stand today, labour as the antagonist of capital is forced to defend its interests not with one but with both hands tied behind its back. One tied by forces openly hostile to labour and the other by its own reformist party and trade union leadership".[1] And I concluded my reasoning with these lines:

> Under these conditions the alternative facing the labour movement is either to resign itself to the acceptance of such constraints, or to take the necessary steps to untie its own hands, no matter how hard that course of action might be. For nowadays the former reformist leaders of labour openly admit, as Tony Blair did it in a speech delivered in Derby appropriately on April Fool's day, that "The Labour party is *the party of modern business and industry in Britain*".[2] This represents the final phase of the total betrayal of everything belonging to the old social democratic tradition that could be betrayed... The only question is, how long will the class of labour allow itself to be treated as April's Fool, and how long can the strategy of

capitulating to big business be pursued beyond *the coming Pyrrhic electoral victory".*[3]

As we all know, more than ten years have now passed in Britain since the establishment of the "New Labour" Government. The Pyrrhic electoral victory turned out to be worse than possibly even the worst expectations. All of the anti-labour legislative measures of the most reactionary Conservative Government in Britain for decades—Margaret Thatcher's Government, once loudly denounced by the Labour Party in opposition—have been retained by the new government, with the full complicity of the dominant trade union leadership. At the same time some representatives of big business were rewarded not only with significant economic and financial advantages but even with long lasting ministerial and key advisory positions. But perhaps the most disastrous aspect of the "New Labour" Government is the total servilism—and cynicism, wrapped up for public consumption in unctuous hypocrisy—with which it participated, and continues to participate, in genocidal American military adventures, ignoring in the most authoritarian way the protest of even millions of people demonstrating against them. And it makes no difference in this respect whether the Washington orders are received from the "brotherly" Democratic President Bill Clinton or from the head of the most extreme Republican Administration in history, George W Bush. The only consistency that seems to be required is conformity to the transatlantic orders with appropriate servilism and hypocrisy even when the stakes concern undeniable and growing military destruction.

There is a tendency to ascribe the deplored characteristics of social and political development to personal aberrations and betrayals, wishfully anticipating their solution by some future changes in personnel. This is to some extent understandable because personalising matters in that way remains within the framework of explanation to which the people involved are well accustomed. However, calling for a very different line of approach does not mean denying the role of personal aberrations and betrayals in the field of politics. There are far too many rewards which induce politicians to side with the perpetuation of the established order. Such rewards are inseparable from the alienated character of institutionalised politics in our societies, divorced from the great masses of the people and thereby usurping with great ease the role of decision making. But precisely for that reason of systemic determination it would be quite wrong to attribute the persistent negative political developments primarily to personal betrayals, even if at a certain level of political interchanges their significant contributory role is undeniable. For the uniformity with which these characteristics persist in the capitalist societies underlines the need for a very different explanation. The underlying contradictions and determinations are much more serious than what could be made intelligible simply in personal terms.

When we talk about the undoubtedly most problematical development of the reformist labour movement in the twentieth century, it is necessary to face up to the grave structural problems of our "democratic politics" if we want to find a more plausible explanation to what continues to go hopelessly wrong as regards genuine socialist expectations than the suggested question begging "personality" failure and associated corruption. These structural problems reach back to a much earlier stage in the historical past than the twentieth century and, worse than that, continue to exercise their negative impact today more strongly than ever before. It is absolutely necessary to face up to them. For the deep-seated *social determinants* that *favour* the appearance of capital's willing personifications in positions of command also in the labour movement—no matter how clearly identifiable—must be not only convincingly accounted for. They must be also objectively *countered* on a lasting basis if we want to avoid their reappearance at the next round of more or less routinised personnel changes within the framework of the parliamentary political system which regulates our "democratic societies".

Unfortunately in this regard we encounter two major difficulties opposed to the necessary radical critique. First, the customary *self-referentiality* of political discourse, offering both diagnoses and remedies strictly confined to the institutionalised setting of political decisions and ignoring the way in which the fundamental material interests of the ruling social metabolic order determine the outcome of the renewed conflicts and antagonisms. (Naturally, the one-sided personalisation of political betrayals is well in tune with the self-referentiality of politics.) And the second major difficulty arises from the way in which the parliamentary system itself is treated in traditional political discourse. For it tends to be proclaimed as the necessary centre of reference of all legitimate change. Criticism is admissible only in relation to some of its minor details, envisaging potential correctives precisely for the purpose of patching up to some extent the established framework of parliamentary politics, even when its increasing vacuity cannot be denied,[4] and leaving the structurally well entrenched political decision making process itself as before. In other words, parliament as such is treated as a taboo, excluding the legitimacy of advocating the institution of a viable radical alternative to the parliamentary entrapment of working class politics. This is a very grave matter. For without instituting a radical alternative to parliamentarism there can be no hope of extricating the socialist movement from its present situation, at the mercy of capital's willing personifications even in its own ranks.

2.

THE NECESSARY alternative to parliamentarism is closely linked to the question of real *participation*, defined as the fully autonomous self-management of their society by the freely associated producers in every domain, well beyond the (for some time obviously necessary) mediatory constraints of the modern political state.

On the face of it the major difference between our concern with participation and the necessity to find a viable alternative to parliamentarism is that whereas full participation is an absolutely fundamental and permanent regulative principle of socialist interrelations—in no matter how advanced and how distant a form of socialist society—the need for producing a strategically sustainable alternative to parliamentarism is immediate, unavoidably and with urgency facing us. However, this is only the most obvious aspect of the important problem of how to liberate the socialist movement from the straitjacket of bourgeois parliamentarism. It has another dimension as well, concerned with the much broader and ultimately no less unavoidable challenge which is usually referred to in the socialist literature as *"the withering away of the state"*.

The apparently prohibiting difficulties of that vital Marxian project apply with equal relevance and weight to both *participation* and to the enduring way of unifying the material reproductive and the political sphere as the envisaged radical alternative to *parliamentarism*. Indeed, when we consider the historic task of making real "the withering away of the state", self-management through full participation and the permanently sustainable overcoming of parliamentarism by a positive form of substantive—in opposition to politically confined formal/legal—decision making are inseparable.

As an issue the necessity to institute a valid alternative to parliamentarism arises from the historically specific political institutions of our own time, as they have been transformed—much for the worse, to the point of becoming a force of paralysis, instead of potential advancement—in the course of the twentieth century, bitterly disappointing all hope and expectations once held by the radical socialist movement. For the ironical and in many ways tragic result of long decades of political struggle within the confines of capital's self-serving political institutions turned out to be that under the now prevailing conditions the working class has been *totally disenfranchised* in all of the capitalistically advanced and not so advanced countries. This condition is marked by the full conformity of the various organised working class representatives to the "rules of the parliamentary game". Naturally, the parliamentary game is massively prejudged against the organised force of labour by the long established and constantly renewed power relations of capital's materially and ideologically most effective rule over the social order in its entirety. In this sense social democratic capitulation, while claiming to represent the "real interests of the working class", in fact fully completed the vicious circle of this process of total disenfranchising from which there can be no escape without radically overcoming—in a truly sustainable way—the historically anachronistic parliamentary system itself.

The contrast between the actually existing conditions of our time and the promises of the past could not be greater.

Particularly when we remind ourselves of the political developments of the last third of the nineteenth century and labour's
hope invested in them. As we all know, well before that time
the working class movement appeared on the historical stage
and made its first advances as an *extra-parliamentary movement*.
The last third of the nineteenth century, however, produced a
significant change in that respect, with the formation and
strengthening of *mass* working class parties which began to
orient themselves, in their majority, toward the gradual conquest of the political domain by electoral means, so as to
introduce—through consensual legislative intervention—the
required far-reaching and lasting structural reforms in society
as a whole. As a matter of fact, as time went by, the mass parties
of the working class were able to show some spectacular successes in strictly electoral terms, adopting and nourishing, as a
result, the most problematical anticipation of a corresponding
success, *"in due course"*, also in the material power relations of
society. This is how social democratic reformism became dominant in the working class parties of the most powerful
capitalist countries, marginalising at the same time the radical
wing of the labour movement for several decades.

But the "due course" hoped for never arrived and never
could arrive. Instituting a radically different social order within
the self-serving parameters of capital's social metabolic control
could be from the very beginning nothing more than a *contradiction in terms*. Whether the advocated political and social
strategy was called, by Bernstein and his followers, *"evolutionary socialism"*, or *"conquering the commanding heights of the
economy"* by Harold Wilson and others, the long promised land
repeatedly proclaimed by such strategies could only be the
leisurely march toward the *never-nowhere-land* of a fictitious
future, in the end clamorously and completely *left behind* by
British "New Labour"—as well as by German and many other
Social democratic parties all over the world—without ever getting nearer to it even by one inch.

Moreover, what makes this problem even graver is that some
of the most important and also electorally successful parties of
the radical left, constituted within the framework of the Third
International, in forceful explicit condemnation of the irretriev-
able historical failure of the Social democratic Second

International, followed—this time really *in due course*—the same disastrous path as the parties which they had strongly denounced and dismissed earlier. It is enough to think in this respect of the "parliamentary road to socialism" pursued by the Italian and the French Communist Parties. Indeed, the Italian Communist party (once the party of no less a revolutionary figure than Antonio Gramsci)—after indulging in the other fantasy-strategy of "the Great Historic Compromise", disregarding or perhaps genuinely forgetting that it takes at least two to make a real compromise, otherwise one can only compromise oneself—rebaptised as the "Democrats of the Left", so as to fully accommodate itself to the service of capital's "democratic" social order. And when we recall that Mikhail Gorbachev, the General Secretary of the Soviet party—a party once upon a time Lenin's own party—presumed to himself the power and the right to *dissolve the party by decree*, and could actually get away with such an authoritarian move in the name of "glasnost" and democracy, that should be a clear indication that something fundamentally wrong must be redressed in these matters. Nostalgia of the past is not going to offer any solution to the underlying issues.

All this is not said "in hindsight": an expression customarily used in order to deflect criticism and justify the failed strategies of the past, together with the role undertaken by the people who were responsible for imposing them, as if there could be no alternative to following such course of action until the "hindsight"—even now sidelined and disqualified with self-justifying sarcasm—appeared on the horizon. The historically documented real state of affairs could not be more different. For the most far-sighted and profoundly committed advocates of the radical socialist alternative, who were active at the time when the fateful derailment of the organised socialist movement was beginning to gather pace—Lenin and Rosa Luxemburg—clearly diagnosed the unfolding dangers, demonstrating not in hindsight but right then the theoretical and political vacuity of the unfulfillable "evolutionary" prescriptions. And when at an even earlier stage of this process of ultimate capitulatory integration into the bourgeois parliamentary system Marx sounded his unmistakeable warning, in his *Critique of the Gotha Programme*, his insistence that there should be no compromise about principles had to remain a voice in the wilderness.

The forces of organised labour had to make their own experience, however bitter in the end such experience turned out to be. For a long historical period ahead there seemed to be no alternative to following the elusive promise of "the line of least resistance" by the great majority of the labour movement. The promises and temptations of solving the highly complex problems of society through the relatively simple processes of parliamentary legislation were too great to be ignored or bypassed until bitter experience itself could reveal that the structurally entrenched and enforced inequality of the material power relations in capital's favour had to prevail also in the institutionalised political setting, notwithstanding the ideology of—in reality strictly *formal*, and never *substantive*—"democratic choice" and electorally safeguarded "equality". In fact the objectively secured institutional entrapment of labour was further complicated by the corruptive impact of the electoral machinery and the "majority seeking" apologetic ideology associated with it. As Rosa Luxemburg characterised these aspects of the problem a long time ago:

> parliamentarism is the breeding place of all the opportunist tendencies now existing in the Western Social Democracy... [it] provides the soil for such illusions of current opportunism as overvaluation of social reforms, class and party collaboration, the hope of pacific development toward socialism, etc... With the growth of the labour movement, parliamentarism becomes a springboard for political careerists. That is why so many ambitious failures from the bourgeoisie flock to the banners of the socialist parties... [The aim is to] *dissolve* the active, class conscious sector of the proletariat in the *amorphous mass of an "electorate"*.[5]

Naturally, the perversely self-justifying ideology of the pretended democratic respect for the mythical "electorate" could be conveniently used for the purpose of arbitrarily, and often corruptly, controlling the political parties themselves and nullifying the possibility of instituting even minor "gradual reform", as the depressing historical record of the twentieth century clearly demonstrated, resulting in the complete disenfranchising of the working class. It was therefore by no means accidental that attempts to introduce major social changes—in the last fifteen years in Latin America, for instance, notably in Venezuela and now in Bolivia—were coupled with a forceful critique of the parliamentary system and the establishment of Constitutional Assemblies as the first step toward the advocated far-reaching transformations.

3.

SIGNIFICANTLY ENOUGH, the critique of the parliamentary system is almost as old as parliament itself. The exposure of its incurable limitations from a radical perspective did not begin with Marx. We find it powerfully expressed already in Rousseau's writings. Starting from the position that sovereignty belongs to the people and therefore it cannot be rightfully alienated, Rousseau argued that for the same reasons it cannot be legitimately turned into any form of representational abdication:

> The deputies of the people, therefore, are not and cannot be its representatives; they are merely its stewards, and can carry through no definitive acts. Every law the people has not ratified in person is null and void—is, in fact, not a law. The people of England regards itself as free; but it is grossly mistaken; it is free only during the election of members of parliament. As soon as they are elected, slavery overtakes it, and it is nothing. The use it makes of the short moments of liberty it enjoys shows indeed that it deserves to lose them.[6]

At the same time Rousseau also made the important point that although the power of legislation cannot be divorced from the people even through parliamentary representation, the administrative or 'executive' functions must be considered in a very different light. As he had put it: "in the exercise of the legislative power, the people cannot be represented; but in that of the executive power, which is only the force that is applied to give the law effect, it both can and should be represented".[7] In this way Rousseau had put forward a much more practicable exercise of political and administrative power than what he is usually credited with or indeed is accused of by his detractors even on the left.

In the tendentious misrepresentation of Rousseau's position both of the vitally important principles of his theory, usable in a suitably adapted form also by socialists, have been disqualified and thrown overboard. Yet the truth of the matter is that, on the one hand, the power of fundamental decision making should never be divorced from the popular masses. At the same time, on the other hand, the fulfilment of specific administrative and executive functions in all domains of the social reproductive process can indeed be *delegated* to members of the given community, provided that it is done under rules autonomously set by and properly controlled at all stages of the substantive decision making process by the associated producers.

Thus the difficulties do not reside in the two basic principles themselves as formulated by Rousseau but in the way in which they must be related to capital's material and political control of the social metabolic process. For the establishment of a socialist form of decision making, in accordance with the principles of both inalienable rule-determining power (ie *the "sovereignty" of labour not as a particular class but as the universal condition of society*) and delegating specific roles and functions under well defined, flexibly distributed and appropriately supervised, rules would require entering and radically restructuring capital's antagonistic material domain. A process which would indeed have to go well beyond what could be successfully regulated by considerations derived from Rousseau's principle of inalienable popular sovereignty and its delegatory corollary. In other words, in a socialist order the legislative process would have to be fused with the production process itself in such a way that the necessary *horizontal division of labour*[8] should be appropriately complemented by a system of self-determined *co-ordination* of labour, from the local to the global levels.

This relationship is in sharp contrast to capital's pernicious *vertical division of labour*[9] which is complemented by the "separation of powers" in an alienated and on the labouring masses unalterably superimposed "democratic political system". For the vertical division of labour under the rule of capital necessarily affects and incurably infects every facet also of the horizontal division of labour, from the simplest productive functions to the most complicated balancing processes of the legislative jungle. The latter is an ever denser legislative jungle not only because its endlessly multiplying rules and institutional constituents must play their vital part in keeping firmly under control the actually or potentially challenging behaviour of recalcitrant labour, watchful over limited labour disputes as well as safeguarding capital's overall rule in society at large. Also, they must somehow reconcile at any particular temporal slice of the unfolding historical process—to the extent to which such reconciliation is feasible at all—the separate interests of the plurality of capitals with the uncontrollable dynamics of the totality of social capital tending toward its ultimate self-assertion as a global entity.

Naturally, the fundamental changes required for securing and safeguarding the socialist transformation of society cannot be accomplished *within* the political domain as constituted and ossified during the last four hundred years of capitalist development. For the unavoidable challenge in this respect necessitates the solution of a most bewildering problem. Namely, that capital is the *extra-parliamentary force par excellence* of our social order, and yet at the same time *completely dominates parliament* from the outside while pretending to be simply a part of it, professedly operating in relation to the alternative political forces of the working class movement on a *fully equitable* basis.

Although in its impact this state of affairs is profoundly misleading, our concern is not simply a question of deceptive appearance to which the political representatives of labour personally fall victim. In other words, it is not a condition from which the now deceived people could be in principle personally extricated through the proper ideological/political enlightenment, without any need for radically changing the well entrenched social reproductive order as a whole. Regrettably, it is much more serious than that. For the false appearance itself arises from *objective structural determinations*, and it is constantly reinforced by the dynamics of the capital system in all of its transformations.

4.

IN ONE sense the underlying problem can be briefly characterised as the historically established *separation of
politics*—pursued in parliament and in its various institutional
corollaries—from society's *material reproductive dimension*, as
the latter is embodied and practically renewed in the multiplicity of productive enterprises. As a matter of *contingent historical
development*, capitalism as a social reproductive order had to
unfold and assert itself against the then prevailing feudal political and material reproductive constraints. At first this did not
take the form of a unified political force frontally confronting
the feudal political order. That happened relatively late, at the
particular historical stage of the victorious bourgeois revolutions in some major countries, by which time the material
ground favouring the capitalistic processes was well advanced
in their societies. The first inroads of capitalist development
were made through the emerging multiplicity of productive
enterprises, free in their local context from the political constraints of feudal serfdom. They were in actuality becoming
more significant in the course of materially conquering an
increasingly more important share of the dynamically changing
overall societal reproduction process.

However, the successful advancement of the material reproductive units by themselves was very far from the end of the
story, despite its one-sided theoretical conceptualisations. For
the political dimension was always present in some form. In
fact it had to play an ever greater role, notwithstanding its
peculiar articulation, the more fully developed the capitalist
system had become. For the great multiplicity of *centrifugal*
material reproductive units had to be brought somehow
together under the all-embracing political command structure
of the capitalist state, so that capital's social metabolic order
should not fall apart in the absence of a cohesive dimension.

The wishful presumption of the all-powerfully regulating
"invisible hand" appeared to be a suitable alternative explanation
to the actually very important role of politics. The illusions necessarily associated with the unfolding capitalistic developments
were well illustrated by the fact that at the point in time when
the system was becoming ever more consolidated and also

politically safeguarded by the capitalist state, after the successful
defeat of the feudal adversary a century earlier in the Civil War
and the "Glorious Revolution", an outstanding figure of classical
political economy, Adam Smith, wanted to ban altogether the
"statesman, council or senate whatever" from significant
involvement in economic affairs, dismissing the very idea of
such involvement as "dangerous folly and presumption".[10] The
fact that Adam Smith adopted this position was well understandable, since he held the view that the capitalist reproductive
order represented *"the natural system of perfect liberty and justice"*.[11]
Accordingly, in a similar conception of the reproductive order
there could be neither *need*, nor an admissible *conceptual space*,
for the regulatory intervention of politics. For, in Smith's view,
politics could only interfere with such a "natural system"—one
said to be fully in tune with the requirements of liberty and justice—in an adverse and detrimental way, since it was already
ideally preordained for the good of all by nature itself and perfectly administered in that sense by the "invisible hand".

What was completely missing from Adam Smith's picture
was the always vital question of actually existing and *inherently
conflictual social power relations* without which the dynamics of
capitalist development cannot be made intelligible at all.
However, the acknowledgement of such conflictual relationship would make absolutely essential to offer an appropriate
form of *political* explanation as well. Understandably, that could
not be offered by the great Scottish economist. For in Smith's
theory the place of social conflictual power relations was taken
by the mythically inflated concept of the *"local situation"*, coupled with the notion of the corresponding particular
enterprises locally owned by the purely self-interested individuals who unconsciously—but nonetheless for the benefit of the
whole of society ideally—managed their productive capital
under the mysterious guidance of the "invisible hand". This
local-oriented individualistic—yet harmoniously all-embracing
and universally beneficial—conception of capital's insuperably
conflictual power relations was very far removed from reality
even in the age of Adam Smith himself, not to mention its
"globalised" variety today.

The great defect of such conceptions of which there were
many, even in the twentieth century, was their failure to

recognise and theoretically explain the *immanent objective connection*—which always had to prevail despite the deceptive appearance of unalterable separation—between the capital system's material reproductive and political dimension. In fact without the immanent relationship of the two dimensions the established social metabolic order could not possibly function and survive for any length of time.

However, it is equally necessary to underline in the same context that the paradoxical interrelationship of the two vital dimensions of the capital system—deceptive in its appearance but rooted in objective structural determinations—has far-reaching implications also for successfully instituting the socialist alternative. For it is inconceivable to substantively overcome the established order simply through the political overthrow of the capitalist state,[12] let alone by gaining victory over the forces of exploitation within the given framework of parliamentary legislation.

Expecting the solution of the fundamental structural problems primarily through the political overthrow of the capitalist state cannot address on a lasting basis the mystifyingly compartmentalised but necessary connection between the inherited capital system's material reproductive and political dimension. This is why the historically viable radical reconstitution of the indissoluble unity of the material reproductive and the political sphere on a permanent basis is and remains the essential requirement of the socialist mode of social metabolic control.

5.

IGNORING OR disregarding the harsh reality of capital's conflictual power relations, from the earliest stage of the system's emergence to the *"democratic"* present, and above all transubstantiating the authoritarian subjection and ruthless domination of labour within those power relations into the pretended *"equality"* of all individuals, was an unavoidable concomitant of viewing the world from capital's vantage point even in the writings of the greatest and most progressive intellectual figures of the bourgeoisie.

What had to be obliterated by the adoption of capital's vantage point, from the very beginning, was the blood-soaked
history of the *"primitive accumulation"*[13] in which the emergent
new ruling class continued the well secured exploitative practices of the preceding one—the feudal landed property. This
perverse structural domination had to remain the general rule,
even if it had to assume a new form, putting thereby into relief
again the significant *historical continuity* of the varieties of age-
old class oppression and exploitation.

On the common ground of that affinity, appropriately rede-
fined in accord with the nature of capital, the *permanently
necessary presupposition* of the new productive order of "free
labour" had to be forcefully perpetuated, despite the professed
creed of "freedom and equality". The necessary practical presupposition behind the myth of "free labour" was, of course,
the *exclusive proprietorship* of the all-important controlling
means of production by a tiny minority, and the simultaneous—
ultimately by the state *politically safeguarded*—exclusion of
society's overwhelming majority from them. At the same time,
the brutal reality of the materially / reproductively as well as
politically / ideologically enforced exclusion of the overwhelming majority of the people from the controlling powers of the
social order—which could not have been more remote from,
indeed diametrically opposed to, any idea of a genuine "ethical
state"—had to be kept under the seal of deep silence in the self-
images of the new mode of social metabolic control.

This revealing omission and misrepresentation had to be the
case even in the best self-images conceived from capital's self-
serving vantage point. For that is how the mystifying
separation of politics from the material reproductive dimension
could both fulfil its conservative ideological / cultural function
and at the same time be also celebrated as forever unsurpass-
able. Thus Hegel, for instance, offered in his system the most
ingenious and philosophically absolutised separation of the
openly self-serving material reality of "civil society" and the
political "ethical state". And he postulated the latter as the ideal
corrective to the unavoidable defects of "civil society".

Reversing the actual causal order, Hegel mystifyingly depicted
the vital determination of being *self-serving / egotistic* as if it was
directly emanating from the individuals themselves, although

in reality it was immanent to capital's insurmountable material ontological ground. Such a historically constituted ontological ground was in reality *imposed on the individuals* who could not opt out from operating within the framework of the given social metabolic order. Consequently, the individuals had to *internalise* the system's *objective self-expansionary imperative*— without which that system as such could not possibly survive—as if it sprang out of the inner core of their own *nature-determined* personal aims and purposes, as Pallas Athene was supposed to have sprung out of the head of Zeus fully armed. In this way Hegel was able not only to produce a philo-sophically absolutised dualism of capital's social order (its "civil society" and its "ethical political state") but also to glorify at the same time the historical development corresponding to the claimed "realisation of freedom" in it as "the true *Theodicaea*: the justification of God in history".[14]

The critique of these conceptions, in all their varieties, is highly relevant today. For, maintaining the dualistic conception of the relationship between civil society and the political state can only bring disorienting strategies, irrespective of which side of the adopted dualist vision is given precedence over the other in the envisaged course of action. The unreality of parlia-mentary projections we are familiar with is well matched in this respect by the utter fragility of the expectations attached to the idea of resolving our major problems through the postu-lated institutional counter-force of "civil society".

The adoption of such a position can only result in being trapped by a very naive conception of the nature of "civil soci-ety" itself and by a totally uncritical attitude toward a great multiplicity of NGOs which, belying their self-characterisation as "Non-Governmental Organisations", happen to be well capa-ble of happily coexisting with the dominant retrograde state institutions on which they depend for their financial existence. And even when we think of some organisations of far greater importance than the particular NGOs, like the trade unions, the situation is not much better in this regard. Consequently, to treat trade unions, in opposition to political parties, as somehow belonging to "civil society" alone, in virtue of which they can be used against the political state for a profound socialist transfor-mation, is no more than romantic wishful thinking. For in reality the institutional circle of capital is made of the *reciprocal totalisations* of civil society/political state which deeply inter-penetrate and powerfully support one another.

There can be no realistic strategy of socialist transformation without firmly pursuing the realisation of the *unity of the political and the material reproductive dimensions* also in the organisational domain. In fact the great emancipatory potential of the trade unions consists precisely in their capability to assume (at least in principle) a radical political role—well beyond the rather conservative political function which they now, on the whole, tend to fulfil—in a conscious attempt to overcome the fateful separation of labour's *"industrial arm"* (themselves) and its *"political arm"* (the parliamentary parties), split asunder under the capitalist integument of both of them through the acceptance of parliamentary domination by the majority of the labour movement in the course of the last one hundred and thirty years.

The appearance of the working class on the historical stage was only an *inconvenient afterthought* to the parliamentary system. That system was constituted well before the first organised forces of labour attempted to voice in public the vital interests of their class. From capital's standpoint the immediate response to such inconvenient but growing "nui-sance" was the rather untenable rejection and exclusion of labour's political groups concerned. Later, however, a much more adaptable idea was instituted by the more agile political personifications of capital: that of *taming* in some way the forces of labour. It took at first the form of the paternalistic par-liamentary sponsorship of some working class demands by relatively progressive bourgeois political parties, and later the acceptance of the legitimacy of working class parties in parlia-ment itself, though of course in a *strictly circumscribed* form, compelling them to conform to "the democratic rules of the parliamentary game".

Inevitably, this meant to such parties of labour nothing less than "freely consenting" to their own effective *accommodation*, even if they could maintain for a fairly long time the illusion that in the fullness of time they would be able to radically redress the situation through parliamentary action in their own favour. This is how the original, and potentially alternative *extra-parliamentary force of labour* has been turned into a *permanently disadvantaged* parliamentary organisation. Although this course of development could be explained by the obvious weakness of organised labour at the *beginning*, arguing and justifying in this way what had actually happened simply begs the question under the present circumstances in favour of the social democratic parliamentary blind alley. For the *radical alternative of gaining strength* by the forces of the working class through organising and asserting themselves *outside parliament*—in contrast to the defeatist strategy followed for many decades, all the way to the *complete disenfranchising of the working class* in the name of "gaining strength"—cannot be dismissed so light heartedly, as if a truly radical alternative was an *a priori* impossibility. Especially since the need for sustainable extra-parliamentary action is absolutely vital for the future of a radically rearticulated socialist movement.

6.

THE UNREALITY of postulating the sustainable solution of the grave problems of our social order within the formal/legal framework and corresponding constraints of parliamentary politics arises from the fundamental misconception of the structural determinations of capital's rule, as represented in all varieties of theory that assert the dualism of civil society and the political state. The difficulty, insurmountable within the parliamentary framework, is that since capital is *actually* in control of all vital aspects of the social metabolism, *it can afford* to define the separately constituted sphere of political legitimation as a strictly *formal/legal* matter, thereby necessarily excluding the possibility of being legitimately challenged by parliamentary politics in its *substantive* sphere of socioeconomic reproductive operation. Directly or indirectly, capital controls *everything*, including the parliamentary legislative process, even if the latter is supposed to be fully independent from capital in many theories which fictitiously hypostatise the "democratic equality" of all political forces participating in the legislative process. To envisage a very different relationship to the powers of decision making in our societies, now completely dominated by the forces of capital in every domain, it is necessary to radically challenge capital itself as the *overall controller* of social metabolic reproduction.

What makes this problem worse for all those who are look-ing for significant change on the margins of the established political system is that the latter can claim for itself genuine constitutional legitimacy in its present mode of functioning, based on the historically constituted *inversion* of the actual state of the material reproductive affairs. For inasmuch as the capi-talist is not only the "personification of capital" but simultaneously functions also "as the personification of the *social* character of labour, of the *total workshop as such*",[15] the system can claim to represent the vitally necessary productive power of society vis-à-vis the individuals as the basis of their continued existence, incorporating the interest of all. In this way capital asserts itself not only as the *de facto* but also as the *de jure* power of society, in its capacity as the objectively given necessary condition of societal reproduction, and thereby as the constitutional foundation to its own political order.

The fact that the constitutional legitimacy of capital is histor-ically founded on the ruthless expropriation of the conditions of social metabolic reproduction—the means and material of labour—from the producers, and therefore capital's claimed "constitutionality" (like the origin of most constitutions) is unconstitutional, this unpalatable truth fades away in the mist of a remote past. The "*social productive powers* of labour, or *produc-tive powers of social labour*, first develop historically with the specifically capitalist mode of production, hence appear as something *immanent* in the capital-relation and *inseparable* from it".[16] This is how capital's mode of social metabolic reproduction becomes *eternalised and legitimated* as a lawfully unchallengeable system. Legitimate contest is admissible only in relation to some *minor aspects* of the unalterable overall structure. The real state of affairs on the plane of socioeconomic reproduction—ie the actually exercised productive power of labour and its absolute necessity for securing capital's own reproduction—dis-appears from sight. Partly because of the ignorance of the very far from legitimable historical origin of capital's "primitive accu-mulation" and the concomitant, frequently violent, expropriation of property as the precondition of the system's present mode of functioning; and partly because of the mystify-ing nature of the established productive and distributive relations. For "the *objective conditions of labour* do not appear as subsumed under the worker; rather, he appears as subsumed under them. Capital *employs* Labour. Even this relation in its simplicity is a *personification of things and a reification of persons*".[17]

Nothing of this relationship can be challenged and remedied within the framework of parliamentary political reform. It would be quite absurd to expect the abolition of the "*personifi-cation of things and the reification of persons*" by political decree, and just as absurd to expect the proclamation of such an intended reform within the framework of capital's political institutions. For the capital system cannot function without the perverse overturning of the relationship between persons and things: capital's alienated and reified powers which dominate the masses of the people. Similarly, it would be a miracle if the workers who confront capital in the labour process as "isolated workers" could reacquire mastery over the social productive powers of their labour by some political decree, or even by a whole series of parliamentary reforms enacted under capital's order of social metabolic control. For in these matters there can be no way of avoiding the irreconcilable conflict over the mate-rial stakes of "*either/or*".

Capital can neither abdicate its—usurped—social productive powers in favour of labour, nor can it share them with labour, thanks to some wishful but utterly fictitious "political compro-mise". For they constitute the overall controlling power of societal reproduction in the form of "*the rule of wealth over soci-ety*". Thus it is impossible to escape, in the domain of the fundamental social metabolism, the severe logic of *either/or*. For either wealth, in the shape of capital, continues to rule over human society, taking it to the brink of self-destruction, or the society of associated producers learns to rule over alienated and reified wealth, with productive powers arising from the *self-determined* social labour of its individual—but no longer isolated—members.

Capital is the *extra-parliamentary force par excellence* which cannot possibly be politically constrained by parliament in its power of social metabolic control. This is why the only mode of political representation compatible with capital's mode of functioning is one which *effectively denies* the possibility of contesting its *material power*. And precisely because capital is the extra-parliamentary force par excellence, it has nothing to fear from the reforms that can be enacted within its parliamentary political framework. Since the vital issue on which everything else hinges is that "the *objective conditions of labour* do not appear as subsumed under the worker" but, on the contrary, "he appears as subsumed under them", no meaningful change is feasible without addressing this issue both in a form of politics capable of *matching capital's extra-parliamentary powers* and modes of action, and in the domain of *material reproduction*. Thus the only challenge that could sustainably affect the power of capital is one which would simultaneously aim at assuming the system's key productive functions, and at acquiring control over the corresponding political decision making processes in all spheres, instead of being hopelessly constrained by the circular confinement of institutionally legitimated political action to parliamentary legislation.[18]

There is a great deal of—well justified—critique of formerly leftwing political figures and of their now fully accommodating parties in the political debates of the last decades. However, what is problematical about such debates is that by overemphasising the role of personal ambition and failure, they often continue to envisage remedying the situation within the same political institutional framework which in fact greatly favours the criticised "personal betrayals" and the painful "party derailments". Unfortunately, the advocated and hoped for personnel and government changes tend to reproduce the same deplorable results.

All this should not be very surprising. The reason why the now established political institutions successfully resist significant changes for the better is because they are themselves part of the *problem* and not of the *solution*. For in their immanent nature they are the embodiment of the underlying structural determinations and contradictions through which the modern capitalist state—with its ubiquitous network of bureaucratic constituents—has been articulated and stabilised in the course of the last four hundred years.

Naturally, the state was formed not as a one-sided mechanical *result* but through its *necessary reciprocal interrelationship* to the material ground of capital's historical unfolding, as not only being shaped by the latter but also actively shaping it as much as historically feasible under the prevailing—and precisely through that interrelationship also changing—circumstances. Given the insuperably *centrifugal* determination of capital's productive microcosms even at the level of the giant quasi-monopolistic transnational corporations, only the modern state could assume and fulfil the required function of being the overall command structure of the capital system. Inevitably, that meant the complete alienation of the power of overall decision making from the producers. Even the "particular personifications of capital" were (and are) strictly mandated to act in accord with the structural imperatives of their system. Indeed the modern state, as constituted on the material ground of the capital system, is the *paradigm of alienation* as regards the powers of comprehensive / totalising decision making. It would be therefore extremely naïve to imagine that the capitalist state could willingly hand over the alienated powers of systemic decision making to any rival actor who operates within the legislative framework of parliament.

Thus, in order to envisage a meaningful and historically sustainable societal change, it is necessary to submit to a radical critique both the material reproductive and the political interdeterminations of the entire system, and not simply some of the contingent and limited political practices. The combined totality of the material reproductive determinations and the all-embracing political command structure of the state together constitute the overpowering reality of the capital system. In this sense, in view of the unavoidable question arising from the challenge of *systemic* determinations, with regard to both socioeconomic reproduction and the state, the need for a comprehensive political transformation— in close conjunction to the meaningful exercise of society's vital productive functions without which far-reaching and lasting political change is inconceivable—becomes inseparable from the problem characterised as the *withering away of the state*. Accordingly, in the historic task of accomplishing "the withering away of the state", *self-management* through full participation, and the permanently sustainable overcoming of parliamentarism by a positive form of *substantive decision making* are inseparable, as indicated at the beginning of section 2 of this Introduction.

This is a vital concern and not a "romantic faithfulness to Marx's unrealisable dream", as some people try to discredit and dismiss it. In truth the "withering away of the state" refers to nothing mysterious or remote but to a perfectly tangible process which must be initiated right in our own historical time. It means, in plain language, the *progressive reacquisition of the alienated powers of political decision making* by the individuals in their enterprise of moving toward a genuine socialist society. Without the reacquisition of these powers—to which not only the capitalist state but also the paralysing inertia of the *structurally well entrenched material reproductive practices* are fundamentally opposed—neither the new mode of political control of society as a whole by its individuals is conceivable, nor indeed the *non-adversarial* and thereby *cohesive/plannable* everyday operation of the particular productive and distributive units by the self-managing freely associated producers. Radically superseding *adversariality*, and thereby securing the material and political ground of *globally viable planning*—an absolute must for the very survival of humanity, not to mention the potentially enriched self-realisation of its individual members—are synonymous to the *withering away of the state* as an ongoing historical enterprise.

7.

OBVIOUSLY, A transformation of this magnitude cannot be accomplished without the *conscious dedication* of a revolutionary movement to the most challenging historic task of all, capable of being sustained against all adversity, since engaging in it is bound to rouse the fierce hostility of all major forces of the capital system. It is for this reason that the movement in question cannot be simply a type of political party oriented toward securing *parliamentary concessions*, which as a rule turn out to be nullified sooner or later by the extra-parliamentary vested interests of the established order prevailing also in parliament. The socialist movement cannot possibly succeed in the face of the hostility of such forces unless it is rearticulated as a *revolutionary mass movement*, consciously active in *all* forms of political and social struggle: local, country-wide and global/international. A revolutionary mass movement capable of fully utilising the parliamentary opportunities when available, limited though they might be under the present circumstances, and above all not shirking back from asserting the necessary demands of defiant *extra-parliamentary action*.

The development of this movement is very important for the future of humanity at the present juncture of history. For without a strategically oriented and sustained extra-parliamentary challenge the *parties now alternating in government* can continue to function as convenient reciprocal alibis for the structurally necessary failure of the system toward labour, thereby effectively confining the role of class opposition to its present position as an inconvenient but *marginalisable afterthought* in capital's parliamentary system. Thus in relation to both the material reproductive and the political domain, the constitution of a strategically viable socialist extra-parliamentary *mass* movement—in conjunction with the traditional forms of labour's, at present hopelessly derailed, political organisations, which *badly need the radicalising pressure and support* of such extra-parliamentary forces—is a vital precondition for successfully countering the massive extra-parliamentary power of capital.

The role of a revolutionary extra-parliamentary movement is twofold. On the one hand, it has to formulate and organisationally defend the strategic interests of labour as the historically viable social metabolic alternative. The success of that role is feasible only if the organised forces of labour consciously confront and forcefully negate in practical terms the structural determinations of the established *material reproductive* order as manifest in the capital-relation and in the concomitant subordination of labour in the socioeconomic process, instead of more or less complicitously helping to *restabilise capital in crisis*, as invariably happened at important junctures of the reformist past. At the same time, on the other hand, the open or concealed *political* power of capital which now prevails in parliament needs to be, and can be, challenged—even if now only to a limited degree—through the pressure which *extra-parliamentary forms of action* can exercise on the legislative and the executive.

Extra-parliamentary action can be effective only if it consciously addresses the central aspects and systemic determinations of capital, cutting through the maze of fetishistic appearances through which they dominate society. For the established order materially asserts its power primarily in and through the *capital relation*, perpetuated on the basis of the mystifying *inversion* of the actual productive relationship of the hegemonic alternative classes in capitalist society.

As mentioned already, this inversion enables capital to usurp the role of *"producer"* who in Marx's words *"employs labour"*, thanks to the baffling *"personification of things and the reification of persons"*, and thereby legitimates itself as the inalterable precondition for realising the "interest of all". Since the concept of the "interest of all" really matters, even if it is now fraudulently used to camouflage the total denial of its substance to the overwhelming majority of the people by the formal/legal pretences of "justice and equality", there can be no meaningful and historically sustainable alternative to the established social order without radically overcoming the all-embracing capital relation itself. This is a non-postponable *systemic* demand. *Partial demands* can be and should be advocated by socialists if they have a direct or indirect bearing on the absolutely fundamental demand for overcoming the capital relation itself, which goes to the heart of the matter.

This demand is in sharp contrast to what is now allowed to the forces of opposition by capital's faithful ideologists and political figures. Their major criterion for ruling out the possibility of even the important partial demands of labour is precisely whether they have a potential for negatively affecting the stability of the system. Thus, for instance, even local "politically motivated industrial action" is categorically excluded (even outlawed) "in a democratic society", because its pursuit might have negative implications for the normal functioning of the system. The role of *reformist* parties, by contrast, is welcome, because their demands help to restabilise the system in difficult times—through wage-restricting industrial intervention (with the slogan of the "necessity of tightening the belt") and trade-union-curbing political/legislative agreements. Thus their demands contribute to the dynamics of renewed capital expansion, or are at least "neutral" in the sense that at some

point in the future, even if not at the moment of their first for-
mulation, they can be integrated into the stipulated framework
of normality.

The revolutionary negation of the capital system is conceivable only through a strategically sustained and conscious
organisational intervention. While the tendentiously one-sided
dismissal of "spontaneity" by sectarian presumption must be
treated with the criticism it deserves, it is no less harmful to
underrate the importance of *revolutionary consciousness* and the
organisational requirements of its success. The historical failure of
some major parties of the Third International which once professed Leninist and revolutionary aims, like the Italian and the
French Communist parties mentioned above, should not divert
our attention from the importance of *recreating on a much more
secure ground the political organisations* through which the vital
socialist transformation of our societies can be accomplished in
the future. Evidently, a forceful critical reassessment of what
went wrong so far is a most important part of this process of
renewal. What is amply clear right now is that the *disintegrative
descent* of such parties on the slippery slope of *parliamentary
entrapment* offers an important lesson for the future.

Only two comprehensive modes of social metabolic control
are feasible today: capital's class exploitative reproductive
order—imposed at any cost by the "personifications of capital"—which miserably failed humanity, pushing it in our time to
the brink of self-destruction. And the other order, diametrically
opposed to the established one: the social metabolic *hegemonic
alternative* of labour. A society managed by the social individuals
on the basis of *substantive equality* which enables them to develop
their productive human and intellectual potentialities to the full,
in harmony with the metabolic requirements of nature, instead
of being bent on the destruction of nature and thereby also of
themselves, as capital's mode of uncontrollable social metabolic
control is busy doing it right now. This is why under the present
conditions of capital's structural crisis nothing short of the *comprehensive hegemonic alternative* to capital's rule—spelled out as
the dialectical complementarity of particular but *non-marginalis-
able immediate demands* and the *comprehensive objectives of systemic
transformation*—can constitute the valid programme of the *conscious revolutionary organised movement* all over the world.

The crisis of our social order has never been greater than it is today. Its solution is inconceivable without the sustained intervention of revolutionary politics on an appropriate scale. The ruling order cannot manage its affairs, under the conditions of its deepening structural crisis, without adopting ever more repressive authoritarian measures against the forces opposed to the ongoing destructive trends of development and without the engagement of its dominant imperialist powers by now even in genocidal military adventures. It would be the greatest of illusions to imagine that a socioeconomic and political order of this kind is reformable in the interest of labour when it firmly resisted the institution of all significant change advocated by the reformist movement throughout its long history. For now the margin of accommodatory adjustments is getting narrower in view of the uncontrollable global interrelationship of capital's contradictions and antagonisms. Thus:

> In view of the fact that the most intractable of the global capital system's contradictions is the one between the *internal unrestrainability* of its economic constituents and the now inescapable *necessity of introducing major restraints*, any hope for finding a way out of this vicious circle under the circumstances marked by the activation of capital's absolute limits must be vested in the *political dimension* of the system. Thus in the light of recent legislative measures which already point in this direction, there can be no doubt that the full power of the state will be activated to serve the end of squaring capital's vicious circle, even if it means subjecting all potential dissent to *extreme authoritarian constraints*. Equally, there can be no doubt that whether or not such a 'remedial action' (in conformity to the global capital system's structural limits) will be successfully pursued, despite its obvious *authoritarian character and destructiveness*, will depend on the working class's ability or failure to *radically rearticulate the socialist movement as a truly international enterprise*.[19]

Without the adoption of a viable socialist international perspective the labour movement cannot acquire its much required strength. In this respect the critical reassessment of the history of the past Internationals is no less important than the radical critique of the "parliamentary road to socialism". In fact the unfulfilled promises of these two strategic approaches are closely connected. In the past the failure to realise the necessary conditions of success in one of them deeply affected the prospects of the other, and vice versa. On the one hand, without a strong self-assertive international socialist movement there was no chance of making the socialist perspective prevail in the national parliaments. At the same time, on the other hand, the overwhelming dominance of capital in the national setting, and the ensuing accommodation of internationally most inadequately organised labour to the given parliamentary constraints and to the nationalistic temptations (clamorously highlighted by the capitulation of the social democratic parties to their national bourgeoisie at the outbreak of the First World War), there could be no question of turning the radical Internationals into a cohesive and strategically effective organised force.

Thus the unhappy history of the radical Internationals was by no means accidental. It was connected with their unrealistic assumption of the necessity of a *doctrinal unity* while operating within a political framework which imposed on the overwhelming majority of the labour movement the need for parliamentary accommodation. Indeed it is not inaccurate to say that the pursuit of the two strategic lines of approach alongside one another was in the past mutually exclusive. Accordingly, the necessary change in the future is not feasible without critically addressing the problems of both. Only a conscious and consistently pursued revolutionary movement of labour—asserting itself as the hegemonic alternative to capital's social order—can find a way out of these difficulties.

To be sure, the conscious organised revolutionary movement of labour cannot be contained within the restrictive political framework of parliament dominated by the extra-parliamentary power of capital. Nor can it succeed as a self-oriented sectarian organisation. It can successfully define itself through two vital orienting principles. First, the elaboration of *its own extra-parliamentary programme* oriented toward the comprehensive hegemonic alternative objectives to secure a fundamental systemic transformation. And the second, equally important in strategic organisational terms, its active involvement in the constitution of the necessary *extra-parliamentary mass movement*, as the carrier of the revolutionary alternative capable of changing also the legislative process in a qualitative way. This would represent a major step in the direction of the withering away of the state. Only through these organisational developments directly involving also the great masses of the people can one envisage the realisation of the historic task of instituting labour's hegemonic alternative, in the interest of all-embracing socialist emancipation.

HISTORICAL ACTUALITY OF
THE SOCIALIST OFFENSIVE

THE PRESENT "crisis of Marxism" is largely due to the fact that many of its representatives continue to adopt a *defensive* posture, at a time when we have historically turned an important corner and should engage in a socialist offensive, in keeping with the objective conditions available to us. Indeed, paradoxically, the last twenty five years that increasingly manifested capital's structural crisis—and hence the beginning of the historical offensive in a historical sense—also witnessed a greater than ever willingness of many Marxists to get involved in all kinds of wholesale revision and compromise, in search of new defensive alliances, and nothing really to show as a result of such fundamentally disoriented strategies.

The disorientation in question is, thus, by no means simply ideological. On the contrary, it involves all those institutions of socialist struggle that were constituted under defensive historical circumstances and therefore pursue, under the weight of their own inertia, modes of action which directly correspond to their defensive character. And since the new historical phase inevitably brings with it the sharpening of the social confrontation, the increased defensive reaction of the given institutions (and strategies) of working class struggle is to be expected—but not to be idealised—under the circumstances. Sadly, however, the existing defensive structures and strategies take their own presuppositions for granted and look for solutions which remain anchored to the conditions of the old, and by now surpassed, historical phase.

All this must be stressed as firmly as possible in order to avoid the illusion of easy solutions. For it is not enough to argue in favour of a new ideological/political orientation if the relevant institutional/organisational forms are retained as they exist today. If the current disorientation is the combined manifestation of practical/institutional and ideological factors in their rather inert response to the changed historical circumstances, it would be naive to expect a remedy from what people like to describe as 'ideological clarification'. Indeed, while obviously the two must develop together, the "übergreifendes Moment" in this dialectical reciprocity at the present juncture is the practical/institutional framework of socialist strategy which badly needs restructuring in accordance with the new conditions. These are the problems we have to address in the present volume.

THE NECESSARY OFFENSIVE OF DEFENSIVE INSTITUTIONS

I.I

To say that we are contemporaries to the new historical phase of socialist offensive does not mean in the slightest that from now on the road is smooth and victory near. The phrase "historical actuality" does not imply more than it explicitly states: namely that the socialist offensive confronts us as a matter of *historical* actuality, in contrast to our objective predicament not so long ago, dominated by inescapably defensive determinations. Consciousness does not automatically register social changes, no matter how important, even if *eventually* ("in the last analysis") they are bound to filter through the prevailing channels and modes of political and ideological mediation. But before we reach the stage of the "last analysis", the inertia of the previous mode of response—as articulated in determinate strategies and organisational structures—continues to dominate the way in which people define their own alternatives and margins of action. In this sense, the discourse on "class consciousness" that reproaches the proletariat for "lack of combativity", so long as the instruments and strategies of socialist action remain defensively structured, demonstrates only its own vacuity.

The historical actuality of the socialist offensive in the first instance amounts to no more than the uncomforting negative fact that—due to the changed relation of forces and circumstances—some earlier forms of action ("the politics of consensus", "the strategy of full employment", "the expansion of the welfare state", etc) are objectively blocked, calling for major readjustments in society as a whole. From this initial "brute negativity" it does not follow, however, that the readjustments in question will be positive ones, mobilising the socialist forces in a conscious effort to present themselves as carriers of the alternative social order fit to replace the society in crisis. Far from it. Since the changes required are so drastic, the probability is that people will follow the "line of least resistance" for a considerable time, even if it means suffering significant defeats and imposing major sacrifices upon themselves, rather than readily accept the "leap into the unknown". Only when the options of the prevailing order are exhausted, only then may one expect a *spontaneous* turn towards a radically different solution. (The complete breakdown of the social order in the course of a lost war and the ensuing revolutionary upheavals known from past history well illustrate this point.)

Nevertheless, the difficulties of an adequate socialist response to the changed historical situation do not alter the character of the situation itself, even if they put again into relief the potential conflict between scales of temporality— the immediate and the broad historical framework of events and developments. It is the objective character of the new historic conditions that *ultimately* decides the issue, whatever delays and diversions may follow under the given circumstances. For the truth is that there is a *limit* beyond which forced accommodation and newly imposed sacrifices become intolerable not only *subjectively* for the individuals concerned, but *objectively* as well for the continued functioning of the still dominant social/economic framework. In this sense, and none other, the historical actuality of the socialist offensive— as synonymous with the end of the system of relative improvements through consensual accommodation—is bound to assert itself in the longer run. To assert itself both in the required form of social consciousness and its strategic/instrumental mediation. Even if there can be no guarantees against further disappointments and defeats in the shorter run. For even if it is true that human beings have a boundless capacity to endure absolutely anything imposed upon them, including the worst possible conditions (which is rather doubtful), the resilience of the global system of capital amounts to far less than that today.

1.2

THE OBJECTIVE potentialities of the socialist offensive are inherent in the structural crisis of capital itself, as we shall see in a moment. Now the point is to stress a major contradiction: the absence of adequate political instruments that could turn this potentiality into *reality*. Furthermore, what makes things worse in this respect is that the self-awareness of the organisations concerned is still dominated by past mythologies, depicting the Leninist party, for instance, as the institution of strategic offensive *par excellence*.

To be sure, all instruments and organisations of the working class movement were brought into being in order to overcome some major obstacles on the road to emancipation. In the first instance they were the outcome of spontaneous explosions, and as such they represented a *moment* of attack. Later, as a result of conscious efforts, coordinated structures emerged both in particular countries and on an international scale. But none of them could actually go beyond the horizon of fighting for specific, limited objectives, even if their *ultimate* strategic aim was a radical socialist transformation of the whole of society. One should not forget that Lenin brilliantly—and realistically—defined the Bolsheviks' objectives between February and October 1917 as securing "peace, land and bread" so as to create a viable social base for the revolution. But even in basic organisational terms the "vanguard party" was constituted in such a way that it should be able to *defend* itself against the ruthless attacks of a police state, under the worst possible conditions of clandestinity, from which inevitably followed the imposition of absolute secrecy, a strict command structure, centralisation, etc. If we compare the self-defensively closed structure of this vanguard party with Marx's original idea of producing "communist consciousness on a mass scale"—with its necessary implication of an inherently open organisational structure—we have some measure of the fundamental difference between a defensive and an offensive posture. When the objective conditions implicit in such an aim are in the process of unfolding on a global scale, only then may one realistically envisage the practical articulation of the required organs of socialist offensive.

In truth, Lenin had no illusions in this regard, even if some interpretations tend to rewrite his objectives in the light of retrospective wishful thinking. He based his strategy for breaking the "weakest link of the chain" on his interpretation of the law of uneven development, insisting at the same time that

> *political* revolutions can under no circumstances whatsoever either obscure or weaken the slogan of a *socialist* revolution…which should not be regarded as a *single act*, but as a *period* of turbulent political and economic upheavals, the most intense class struggle, civil war, revolutions and counter-revolutions.[20]

In this spirit, he expected the political revolution of October to open up the "period of turbulent political and economic upheavals", manifest in a whole series of revolutions all over the world, until the conditions of a socialist victory were firmly secured. When the wave of revolutionary upheavals had died down without significant positive results elsewhere, he soberly remarked that one could not hand back power to the Czars, and went on with the job of defending what could be defended under the circumstances. He was originally hoping to combine the political potential of the "weakest link" with the economically mature conditions of the "advanced" capitalist countries. It was the failure of the world revolution that forcibly truncated his strategy, imposing on him the crippling constraints of a desperate defence.

Whereas Lenin always retained his awareness of the fundamental difference between the political and the social (he called it socialist) revolution, even when he was irrevocably forced into defending the bare survival of the political revolution as such, Stalin obliterated this vital distinction, pretending that the *first step* in the direction of a socialist victory represented socialism itself, to be simply followed by stepping onto the "highest stage of Communism" in an encircled country. Naturally, with such an apologetic shift in strategy, the real difference between defensive and offensive structures and developments also disappeared, since everything had to be crudely subordinated to the defence of Stalinism and hailed simultaneously as the greatest possible victory for the socialist revolution in general. And while Lenin, in the absence of the world revolution, saw the task on the whole as a *holding operation* (to be relieved by favourable world developments in due course), Stalin made a virtue out of misery. He transubstantiated the prevailing political response to the given constraints into a general (and thereafter compulsory) *social ideal*, arbitrarily superimposing on all social and economic processes the voluntaristic practice of trying to solve problems by authoritarian *political dictates*.

Thus, we could witness a big diversion from the original intentions not only in terms of the fundamental objectives but also with respect to the corresponding institutional and organisational forms. Marx's overall conception had for its strategic objective the comprehensive social revolution, in terms of which men must change "from top to bottom the conditions of their industrial and political existence, and consequently their whole manner of being".[21] Accordingly, the forms and instruments of the struggle had to match the essentially *positive* character of the undertaking as a whole, instead of being blocked at the *negative* phase of a *defensive* action. This is why Marx, addressing himself to a group of workers, reminded them that they should not content themselves with the negativity of "retarding the downward movement" when the task consisted in "changing its direction"; that they should not apply "palliatives" when the problem was how to "cure the malady". And he went on to make the general point that it was not enough to negatively / defensively engage in the

> unavoidable *guerilla fights* incessantly springing up from the never ceasing encroachments of capital or changes of the market.[22]

However, when it came to spelling out the *positive* side of the equation, under the prevailing conditions of capital's relative underdevelopment—still far from its real barriers and structural crisis—he could only point to the fact of an ongoing process of objective development, but to no tangible institutional and strategic mediations for turning that process to a lasting advantage. As he put it, the workers "ought to understand that, with all the miseries it imposes upon them, the present system simultaneously engenders the *material conditions* and the social forms necessary for an economical reconstruction of society".[23] Thus he was able to indicate a positive ally in the maturing material conditions of society, but he could go no further than that. Insisting as he did more than once in the same lecture that "guerilla war" defensively fights only the effects of the system, he could only offer the metaphor of a "lever" to be used for a fundamental change, in no way identifying where and how that lever might be inserted into the strategic centre of the negated system so as to be able to produce the advocated radical transformation.

It would have been a miracle, had it been otherwise. For the socialist movement, after the first—more or less spontaneous—explosions and attacks born out of despair, found itself in a situation of setting itself very limited targets, in response to the challenges it had to face in the context of particular national confrontations, against the background of capital's global expansion and dynamic development. Accordingly, the First International soon experienced great difficulties which eventually led to its disintegration. And no amount of retrospective mythology can turn even the Paris Commune into a major socialist offensive: not simply because it was brutally defeated, but primarily in view of the fact strongly stressed by Marx himself that it was not socialist at all.[24] Naturally, the debates concerning the Gotha programme and the strategic orientation of the German working class movement were very much under the shadow of the same defensive determinations. The objective conditions for envisaging even the bare possibility of a hegemonic offensive were nowhere in sight, and in their absence the severe limitations of the feasible organisational forms and strategies were also pushed into relief. This is why Marx, after defining the necessary conditions of a successful socialist revolution in terms of "the positive development of the means of production", unhesitatingly declared as late as 1881:

> It is my conviction that the critical juncture for a new International Workingmen's Association has not yet arrived and for this reason I regard all workers' congresses, particularly socialist congresses, insofar as they are not related to the *immediate* given conditions in this or that *particular nation*, as not merely useless but harmful.

They will always fade away in innumerable stale gener-
alised banalities.[25]

Needless to say, the Second International did not bring any
improvement in this respect. On the contrary, through its
"economism" it miserably capitulated to the dominant
social/economic determinations of the overall defensive
predicament. It substituted the pedestrian practice of "gradual
change" to the requirements of a comprehensive strategy,
directly translating at the same time its vision of defensive
capitulation into the ossified organisational structure of a
"Social Democracy" corruptly wedded to capitalist parliamentary manipulation. Well in keeping with that, the postwar
period of capitalist expansion—hailed by many as the permanent solution of capital's contradictions, as well as the
structural integration of the working class—found its most
enthusiastic spokesmen and administrators in this pseudo-
socialist movement of social democratic capitulation.

Contrary to the Second International—which, in a sense, is
still with us today—the historical moment of the Third
International was a relatively brief one. The revolutionary wave
in the closing stages of the First World War gave it a big original impetus, but hardly twenty months after its founding
Congress Lenin had to admit that:

It was evident that the revolutionary movement would
inevitably slow down when the nations secured peace.[26]

Significantly, the same speech that acknowledged the passing of the revolutionary wave in the West, heavily
concentrated on the question of economic concessions to capitalist countries, approvingly quoting Keynes about the
importance of Russian raw materials for the reconstitution
and stabilisation of the global economy of capital and consciously adopting it as the strategy of the foreseeable future.
By the time the strategists of the German "March Action"
embarked on their voluntaristic "offensive", the dice of objective determinations were heavily loaded against any such
offensive, putting a tragic seal on the fate of revolutionary
socialist movements for a long time to come.

The world of capital weathered also the storm of its "Great Economic Crisis" of 1929-33 with relative ease, without having to face a major hegemonic confrontation from socialist forces despite the mass suffering caused by this crisis. For the fact is that "Great" as this crisis was, it was very far from being a *structural* crisis, leaving an ample number of options open for capital's continued survival, recovery and stronger than ever reconstitution on an economically sounder and broader basis. Retrospective political reconstructions tend to blame personalities and organisational forces for such recovery, particularly with respect to the success of fascism. Yet, whatever the relative weight of such political factors, one should not forget that they must be assessed against the background of an essentially defensive historical phase. It is pointless to rewrite history with the help of counter-factual conditionals, whether they concern the rise of fascism or anything else. For the fact that really matters is that at the time of the crisis of 1929-33 capital actually did have the *option of fascism* (and similar solutions) which it no longer possesses today. And objectively that makes a world of difference as far as the possibilities of defensive and offensive action are concerned.

1.3

GIVEN THE way in which they had been constituted—as integral parts of a complex institutional framework—the organs of socialist struggle could win individual battles, but not the war against capital itself. For the latter a fundamental restructuring would be required, so that they complement and intensify each other's effectiveness, instead of weakening it through the "division of labour" forced upon them by capital's "circular" institutionality within which they originated. The two pillars of working class action in the West—parties and trade unions—are in fact inseparably linked to a third member of the overall institutional setting: Parliament, through which the circle of civil society/political state is closed and becomes that paralysing "magic circle" from which there seems to be no escape. To treat trade unions, together with other (far less important) sectoral organisations, as somehow belonging to "civil society" alone, in virtue of which they can be used against the political state for a profound socialist transformation, is no more than romantic wishful thinking. For the institutional circle of capital in reality is made of the *reciprocal totalisations* of civil society/political state which deeply interpenetrate and powerfully support one another. Thus, it would take much more than knocking down one of the three pillars—parliament, for instance—to produce the necessary change.

The problematic side of the prevailing institutional framework is tellingly captured by expressions like "trade union consciousness", "party bureaucracy", and "parliamentary cretinism", to name but one in each category. Parliament, in particular, has been the target of many a justified criticism, and up to the present time there is no satisfactory socialist theory as to what to do with it beyond the conquest of power: a fact that loudly speaks for itself. While the classics of Marxism fought against "indifference to politics" and the equally sectarian advocacy of "boycotting parliament", they did not envisage an "intermediary stage" (which might in fact be a very long historical phase). A stage that in a meaningful sense retains at least some important features of the inherited parliamentary framework while the long-drawn-out process of radical restructuring is accomplished on the required comprehensive scale. Marx, for instance, raised this possibility by implication, in an aside arising in the context of revolutionary change tied to the use of force as a rule. This is how he tackled the problem in an important but little known speech:

> The worker will some day have to win political supremacy in order to organise labour along *new lines*: he will have to defeat the *old policy* supporting *old institutions*...
>
> But we have by no means affirmed that this goal would be achieved by identical means. We know of the *allowances* we must make for the *institutions, customs and traditions* of the various countries; and we do not deny that there are countries such as America, England, and I would add Holland if I knew your institutions better, where the working people may achieve their goal by *peaceful means*. If that is true, we must also recognise that in most of the continental countries it is force that will have to be the lever of

revolutions; it is *force* that we shall some day have to resort
to in order to establish a reign of labour.[27]

It is arguable whether the issue at stake is simply a question
of "allowances" that must be made for some inherited constraints: the importance of parliament is far too great to be
dealt with in passing and in the company of "customs and traditions". Understandably, in Marx's conception of politics as
radical negation, parliament usually appears in its almost
grotesque negativity, summed up with the dictum: "To delude
others and by deluding them to delude yourself—this is *parliamentary wisdom* in a nutshell! Tant mieux!"[28] Is it really "so
much the better" or is it "so much the worse"?

Since parliament profoundly affects all institutions of socialist struggle which happen to be closely linked to it, surely it
must be so much the worse. And if you add to this fact the consideration—raised by Marx as a serious historical possibility,
and not as an empty gesture of factionalist party propaganda—
that revolutionary change may use *peaceful means* as its vehicle,
in that case the imperative of radically reorienting "parliamentary wisdom" for the realisation of socialist aims becomes so
much more pressing.

The experience of the societies of "actual socialism" clearly
shows that it is impossible to demolish just one of the three pillars of the inherited institutional framework, since one way or
another also the remaining two go with it. This is fairly obvious
when we think of the purely nominal existence of the trade
unions in these societies, just as the experience of Poland and
the resurfacing of bitterly independent trade unionism from
limbo in the form of "Solidarity" made it amply clear that balancing society on top of the one remaining pillar is totally
untenable in the longer run. Less obvious, though, is what
happens to the party itself in the aftermath of the conquest of
power. While it may retain some organisational features of
Lenin's "vanguard party" as constituted under the conditions of
illegality and struggle for mere survival against the Czarist
police state, by becoming the unchallengeable ruler of the new
state it ceases to be a Leninist party and becomes in fact the
Party-State, imposing and also suffering all the consequences
which this change necessarily carries with it. Thus, transfer of

power from one set of individuals to another (a laughably com-
monplace occurrence in the parliamentary framework), or
even a partial shift in policy under changed circumstances,
becomes extremely difficult, if not impossible.

THE NATURE of the overall institutional framework determines
also the character of its constituent parts, and vice-versa, the
particular "microcosms" of a system always exhibit the essential
characteristics of the "macrocosm" to which they belong. In this
sense no change can become other than purely ephemeral in
any particular constituent, unless it can fully reverberate
through all channels of the total institutional complex, thus ini-
tiating the required changes in the whole system of reciprocal
totalisations and interdeterminations. To win "guerilla fights",
as Marx insisted, was not enough, since they could ultimately be
neutralised or even nullified by the assimilative and integrative
power of the ruling system. The same was true of winning *individual battles* when the issue was ultimately decided in terms of
the conditions of winning the *war* itself.

  This is why the historical actuality of the socialist offensive
is of an immense significance. For under the new conditions of
capital's structural crisis it becomes possible to win much
more than some great (but in the end badly isolated) *battles*
like the Russian, Chinese and Cuban revolutions. At the same
time, there can be no question of minimising the painful character of the process involved, requiring major strategic
adjustments and correspondingly radical institutional/organi-
sational changes in all areas and across the whole spectrum of
the socialist movement.

2.

FROM CYCLIC TO STRUCTURAL CRISIS

2.1

As MENTIONED before, the crisis of capital we are experiencing today is an all-embracing structural crisis. There is nothing special, of course, in linking capital to crisis. On the contrary, crises of varying intensity and duration happen to be capital's *natural* mode of existence: ways of progressing beyond its immediate barriers and thus extending with ruthless dynamism its sphere of operation and domination. In this sense, the last thing that capital could envisage is a *permanent* supersession of all crises, even if its ideologists and propagandists frequently dream about (or indeed claim the achievement of) nothing less than that.

The *historical* novelty of today's crisis is manifest under four main aspects:

(1) its *character* is *universal*, rather than restricted to one particular sphere (eg financial, or commercial, or affecting this or that particular branch of production, or applying to this rather than that type of labour, with its specific range of skills and degrees of productivity, etc;

(2) its *scope* is truly *global* (in the most threateningly literal sense of the term), rather than confined to a particular set of countries (as all major crises have been in the past);

(3) its *time scale* is extended, continuous—if you like: *permanent*—rather than limited and *cyclic*, as all former crises of capital happened to be;

(4) its *mode* of unfolding might be called *creeping*—in contrast to the more spectacular and dramatic eruptions and collapses of the past—while adding the proviso that even the most vehement or violent convulsions cannot be excluded as far as the future is concerned: ie when the complex machinery now actively engaged in "crisis-management" and in the more or

less temporary "displacement" of the growing contradictions runs out of steam.

To deny that such machinery exists and that it is powerful, would be extremely foolish. Nor should one exclude or minimise capital's ability to add new instruments to the already vast arsenal of its continued self-defence. Nevertheless, the fact that the existing machinery is being brought into play with increasing frequency and that it proves less and less effective as things stand today, is a fair measure of the severity of this deepening structural crisis.

HERE WE must concentrate on a few constituents of the unfolding crisis. If in the postwar period it has become embarrassingly unfashionable to talk about capitalist crisis—yet another sign of the defensive posture of the labour movement mentioned above—it was not only due to the successful practical operation of the machinery that displaces (through diffusing as well as de-fusing) the contradictions themselves. It was also due to the ideological mystification (from "the end of ideology" to the "triumph of organised capitalism" and "working class integration", etc) which misrepresented the *mechanism of displacement* as a structural remedy and *permanent solution*.

Naturally, when the manifestations of the crisis cannot be hidden any longer, the same ideological mystification that yesterday announced the final solution of all social problems today attributes their reemergence to purely *technological* factors, belching out its apologetic platitudes about "the second industrial revolution", "the collapse of work", "the information revolution", and the "cultural discontents of post-industrial society".

To appreciate the historical novelty of capital's structural crisis, we have to locate it in the historical context of twentieth century social, economic and political developments. But first, it is necessary to make some general points about the criteria of a structural crisis, as well as about the forms in which its solution may be envisaged.

To put it in the simplest and most general terms, a structural crisis affects the *totality* of a social complex, in all its relations with its constituent parts or sub-complexes, as well as with other complexes to which it is linked. By contrast, a non-structural crisis affects only some parts of the complex in question, and thus no matter how severe it might be with regard to the affected parts, it cannot endanger the continued survival of the overall structure.

Accordingly, the displacement of contradictions is feasible only while the crisis is partial, relative and internally manageable by the system, requiring no more than shifts—even if major ones—*within* the relatively autonomous system itself. By the same token, a structural crisis calls into question the very existence of the overall complex concerned, postulating its transcendence and replacement by some alternative complex.

The same contrast may be expressed in terms of the limits any particular social complex happens to have in its immediacy, at any given time, as compared to those beyond which it cannot conceivably go. Thus, a structural crisis is not concerned with the *immediate* limits but with the *ultimate* limits of a global structure. The immediate limits may be extended in three different ways:

(a) by modifying some parts of a complex in question;

(b) by changing, as a whole, the system to which the particular sub-complexes belong; and

(c) by significantly altering the relationship of the overall complex to other complexes outside it.

Consequently, the greater the complexity of a fundamental structure and of its relationships with others to which it is linked, the more varied and flexible are its objective possibilities of adjustment and its chances of survival even under extremely severe conditions of crisis. In other words, partial contradictions and "dysfunctions", even if severe in themselves, can be displaced and diffused—within the *ultimate* or *structural limits* of the system—and the countervailing forces or tendencies neutralised, assimilated, nullified, or even turned into an actively sustaining force of the system in question. Hence the problem of reformist accommodation. However, all this should be kept in perspective, in contrast to the grotesquely overstated theories of "working class integration" which were fashionable not so long ago. For the undeniable integration of the leadership of most working class parties and trade unions should not be confused with the hypostatised—but structurally impossible—integration of labour as such into the capital system.

At the same time it must be stressed that when the manifold

options of internal adjustment begin to be exhausted, not even the "curse of interdependence" (which tends to paralyse the forces of opposition) can prevent the ultimate structural disintegration. Naturally, given the inherent character of the structures involved, it is inconceivable to think of such disintegration as a sudden act, to be followed by an equally speedy transformation. The "creeping" but relentlessly advancing structural crisis can only be grasped as a contradictory process of *reciprocal adjustments* (a "war of attrition" of sorts), to be brought to a conclusion only by a long and painful process of *radical restructuring* inevitably tied to its own contradictions.

2.2

As FAR as the world of capital is concerned, the manifestations of the structural crisis can be identified in its various internal dimensions as well as at the level of the political institutions. As Marx had repeatedly stressed, it is in the nature of capital to drive beyond the barriers it encounters:

> The tendency to create the world market is directly given in the concept of capital itself. Every limit appears as a barrier to be overcome. Initially, to subjugate every moment of production itself to exchange and to suspend the production of direct use values not entering into exchange... But from the fact that capital posits every such limit as a barrier and hence gets ideally beyond it, it does not by any means follow that it has really overcome it, and, since every such barrier contradicts its character, its production moves in contradictions which are constantly overcome but just as constantly posited. Furthermore, the universality towards which it irresistibly strives encounters barriers in its own nature, which will, at a certain stage of its development, allow it to be recognised as being itself the greatest barrier to this tendency, and hence will drive towards its own suspension.[29]

In the course of actual historical development capital's three fundamental dimensions—production, consumption and circulation / distribution / realisation—tend to strengthen and expand one another for a long time, providing also the necessary internal motivation for each other's dynamic reproduction on an ever-extended scale. Thus in the first place the *immediate* limitations of each are successfully overcome, thanks to the reciprocal interaction of the others. (Eg the immediate barrier to production is positively superseded by the expansion of consumption, and vice-versa.) In this way, the limits truly appear to be no more than mere barriers to be transcended, and the immediate contradictions are not only displaced but directly utilised as levers for the exponential increase in capital's seemingly boundless power of self-propulsion.

Indeed, there can be no question of a *structural* crisis so long as this vital mechanism of self-expansion (which is simultaneously also the mechanism of internally transcending or displacing contradictions) continues to function. There may be all kinds of crises of varying duration, frequency, and severity directly affecting one of the three dimensions and *indirectly*, until the blockage is removed, the system as a whole, without, however, calling into question the *ultimate limits* of the overall structure. (For instance, the crisis of 1929-33 was essentially a "realisation crisis", at an absurdly low level of production and consumption as compared to the postwar period.)

To be sure, the structural crisis does not originate in some mysterious region of its own: it resides in and emanates from the three internal dimensions mentioned above. Nevertheless, the dysfunctions of each taken separately must be distinguished from the fundamental crisis of the whole which consists in the *systematic blockage* of the vital constituent parts.

It is important to make this distinction because—given the objective interconnections and reciprocal determinations—under specific circumstances even a temporary blockage of *one* of the internal channels may with relative ease drive the whole system to a halt, thus creating the *semblance* of a structural crisis, together with some voluntaristic strategies arising from the misperception of a temporary blockage as a structural crisis. It is worth remembering in this context Stalin's fatefully optimistic evaluation of the crisis of the late 1920s, and its devastating consequences for his policies both internally and on the international plane.

2.3

ANOTHER MISCONCEPTION that must be cleared out of the way is that structural crisis refers to some abstractly *absolute* conditions. This is not so. To be sure, all three fundamental dimensions of capital's continued functioning have their absolute limits which can be clearly identified. (For instance, the absolute limits of production may be expressed in terms of the means and material of production, which in their turn may be further specified as the total collapse of the supply of certain key raw materials, or as the equally total collapse—not just "under-utilisation"—of the available productive machinery, for whatever reason, as, for instance, the irresponsible and reckless misuse of energy resources.) But while such considerations are certainly not irrelevant, they suffer from the avoidance of social specificities (as many environmentalist arguments testify), thereby unnecessarily weakening their own weapons of critique by linking them to doomsday expectations which need *never* materialise.

* Capital's structural crisis which we started to experience in the 1970s relates, in fact, to something far more modest than such absolute conditions. It means simply that the threefold internal dimensions of capital's self-expansion exhibit increasingly greater disturbances. Thus they not only tend to disrupt the normal process of growth but also foreshadow a failure in their vital function of displacing the system's accumulated contradictions.

* The inner dimensions and inherent conditions of capital's self-expansion constituted from the very beginning a *contradictory* unity, and not an unproblematical one, in that one had to "subjugate" the other (as Marx had put it: to "subjugate every moment of production itself to exchange") so as to make the overall complex work. At the same time, so long as the expanded reproduction of each could continue undisturbed—ie so long as it was possible to dig increasingly bigger holes in order to fill the earlier smaller ones with their contents—not only each of the contradictory internal dimensions could be strengthened separately but they could also function together in a "contrapuntal" harmony.

* The situation radically changes, however, when the interests

of each on its own cease to coincide with those of the other even in the last analysis. From that moment on, the disturbances and antagonistic "dysfunctions", rather than being absorbed/dissipated/diffused and de-fused, tend to become *cumulative* and thus *structural*, carrying with them a dangerous blockage in the complex mechanism of *displacing contradictions*. Thus what we are confronted with is no longer simply "dysfunctional" but potentially very explosive. For capital never-ever solved even the smallest of its contradictions.

* Nor could it do so, since by its very nature and inherent constitution capital *thrives* on them (and can safely do so up to a point). Its normal way of dealing with contradictions is to intensify them, to transfer them to a higher level, to displace them to a different plane, to suppress them as long as it is possible to do so, and when they cannot be suppressed any longer, to export them to a different sphere or to a different country. This is why the increasing blockage in displacing and exporting capital's inner contradictions is so dangerous and potentially explosive.

It goes without saying, this structural crisis is not confined to the social/economic sphere. Given the inescapable determinations of capital's "magic circle" earlier referred to, the profound crisis of "civil society" loudly reverberates on the whole spectrum of political institutions. For under the increasingly more unstable socioeconomic conditions, new and much stronger "political guarantees" are needed which cannot be provided by the capitalist state as it stands today. Thus the ignominious demise of the "welfare state" only puts the seal of open admission on what is no less than the *structural crisis of all political institutions* which has been fermenting under the crust of "consensus politics" for well over two decades. What needs to be stressed here is that the underlying contradictions by no means fizzle out in the crisis of *political* institutions but affect the whole of society in a way never experienced before. Indeed, the structural crisis of capital reveals itself as a veritable *crisis of domination* in general.

Anyone who might feel that this sounds too dramatic should just look around, in whatever direction. Is it possible to find any sphere of activity or any set of human relations not affected by the crisis? A hundred and forty years ago Marx could still speak

about "the great civilising influence of capital", emphasising
that through it

> for the first time, nature becomes purely an object for
> humankind, purely a matter of utility; ceases to be recog-
> nised as a power for itself; and the theoretical discovery of
> its autonomous laws appears merely as a ruse so as to sub-
> jugate it under human needs, whether as an object of
> consumption or as a means of production. In accord with
> this tendency, capital drives beyond national barriers and
> prejudices as much as beyond nature worship, as well as all
> traditional, confined, complacent, encrusted satisfactions
> of present needs, and reproductions of old ways of life.[30]

And where does it all lead to? For capital can have no other
objective than its own self-reproduction to which everything
else must be absolutely subordinated, from nature to all human
needs and aspirations.

Thus the civilising influence comes to a devastating end the
moment the ruthless inner logic of capital's expanded self-
reproduction encounters its obstacle in human needs. One
year's military budget in the USA alone amounts (in 1981) to the
figure of 300 billion dollars, (and who knows how much more
in addition to that, under various other budgetary covers),
which defies human comprehension. At the same time the
most elementary social services are subjected to callous cuts: a
true measure of capital's "civilising work" today. Yet, even such
sums and cuts are very far from being sufficient to enable capital to follow its undisturbed course: one of the striking proofs
of the crisis of domination.

The systematic devastation of nature and the continued
accumulation of the powers of ultimate destruction—globally
to the tune of well over one trillion dollars per annum—indicate the frightening material side of capital's absurd logic of
development, together with the complete denial of the elementary needs of countless starving millions: the forgotten side and
receiving end of the wasted trillions. The paralysing human
side of this development is visible not only in the obscenity of
enforced "underdevelopment" but everywhere even in the capitalistically most advanced countries.

The prevailing system of domination is in crisis because its historical *raison d'être* and justification has disappeared, and no amount of manipulation or naked repression can reinvent it. Thus, keeping thousands of millions of people in destitution and starvation when the wasted trillions could feed them *fifty times* over puts the enormity of this system of domination in perspective.

The same is true of those other great human issues which started to mobilise people a relatively short time ago. Sociological literature had produced so many nice fairy tales, for decades, about "generation conflict" (in the true spirit of "the end of ideology", attempting to turn the nasty signs of class contradictions into the noble vicissitudes of timeless generations); now they really have something to write about. However, the prefabricated schemes of psycho/sociological mystification do not fit the real picture. For the so-called "generation conflict" was automatically resolved the moment it was apologetically predicated, in that all "youthful rebellion" was supposed to grow in due course into the sound maturity of mortgage payments and savings for an old-age pension, so as to secure commodity-existence all the way to the grave and beyond, through the eternal reproduction of capital's new "generations". The self-reassuring idea was that whatever difficulties "nature" may present us with—and the notion of 'generations' was supposed to be simply a category of nature—capital will, thankfully, resolve them as a matter of course.

The truth, however, turned out to be the exact opposite, since capital does not resolve but *generates* the real conflict of generations, on an ever-extending scale. Millions of young people are denied the chance of a job in every major capitalist country, unceremoniously obliterating the not so old memory of courtship about "youth culture", while continuing to squeeze every possible drop of profit out of the remnants of such culture. At the same time, millions of older people are also forced to join the dole queues, and millions more are under an immense pressure for "early retirement" from which the most mobile section of contemporary capital—finance capital—can suck some more profit for a while at least. Thus the age-group of the "useful generation" is shrinking to somewhere between 25 and 50, and it is *objectively* opposed to the "unwanted generations" condemned by capital to enforced idleness and the loss of their humanness. And since now the middle generation is squeezed between the "useless young" *and* the "useless old"—until, that is, it becomes itself superfluous, when capital deems so—even the temporal planes of these contradictions become all-confounding.

Typically, the solutions proposed do not even scratch the surface of the problem, underlining that, again, we are confronted with an insoluble inner contradiction of capital itself. For what is really at stake is the role of labour as such in capital's universe once a very high level of productivity is reached. To cope with the contradictions generated thereby, a major upheaval would be needed, affecting not only the immediate conditions of work itself but all facets of social life as well, even the most intimate ones. Capital, by contrast, can only produce the material conditions for the development of the autonomous social individual so as to negate them immediately. It negates them materially at times of economic crises, as well as at the political and cultural levels in the interest of its own continued survival as the ultimate framework of domination.

Since capital can only function by way of contradictions, it both creates the family and destroys it; both produces the economically independent young generation with its "youth culture" and undermines it; both generates the conditions of potentially comfortable old age, with adequate social provisions, and sacrifices them to the interests of its infernal war-machinery. Human beings are both absolutely needed by capital and totally superfluous to it. If it was not for the fact that capital needs living labour for its extended self-reproduction, the nightmare of the neutron-bomb holocaust would certainly come true. But since such "final solution" is denied to capital, we are confronted with the dehumanising consequences of its contradictions and with the growing crisis of the system of domination.

Perhaps the latter is nowhere more obvious than in the intensifying struggle for women's liberation. The economic grounds of the past historical justification of women's oppression have irretrievably been destroyed, and capital's productive advance itself played a central role in this. But again we can see the inherent contradictions. In one sense—

for its own purposes—capital helps to liberate women so as to be able to better exploit them as members of a much more varied and conveniently "flexible" labour force. At the same time it needs to retain their social subordination on another plane—for the uncomplicated reproduction of the labour force and for the perpetuation of the prevalent family structure—so as to safeguard its own domination as the absolute master of the social metabolism itself.

Thus, it clearly emerges that the partial successes can evaporate from one moment to the next—women are among the first to be forced back into unemployment or into miserably remunerated part-time labour—since capital's *overall* interests predominate over the more limited ones. Given the fact that the real stake is the prevailing system of domination and that significant successes in women's liberation are bound to make deep inroads into it, ultimately undermining its viability, anything that cannot be kept strictly within the bounds set by the pursuit of profit must be resisted. At the same time, capital's major involvement in the destruction of all economic justification of women's oppression make it impossible to resolve this problem by way of an *economic* mechanism. (In fact, purely in economic terms, the balance often points in the opposite direction, thus contributing to the sharpening of this contradiction.)

Since the family is the true microcosm of society—fulfilling beyond its immediate functions also the requirements of securing the continuity of property, to which we must also add its role as the basic unit of distribution and its unique ability to act as the "transmission belt" of the prevailing value-structure of society—the cause of women's liberation directly or indirectly affects the totality of social relations, in all their untenability.

The apparent stalemate in this respect at the present time, under the immediate pressures of the economic crisis, is rather deceptive. For looking at it from the perspective of a longer time-scale we can see a dramatic change, in that the *three* generation family we had before the last war has now effectively turned into a *one generation* family: with all its highly beneficial consequences for the expansion of the consumer-economy.

But even that is no longer enough. Hence the contradictory pressures for further changes—although, in fact, we have run out of the possibility of such changes *while* retaining the existing family structure—and the equally great pressures, if not even greater ones, to move in the opposite direction, restoring the old, patriarchal "family values", in the interest of capital's continued survival. It is the simultaneous presence and intensity of forces irrepressibly pulling in ways like this in opposite directions which makes the present, structural crisis of capital a veritable crisis of domination.

2.4

IN COMPARISON to all this, the crisis of 1929-33 was evidently of a very different kind. For no matter how severe and prolonged that crisis was, it affected only a limited number of capital's complex dimensions and mechanisms of self-defence, corresponding to its relatively underdeveloped state at the time with respect to its overall potentialities. But before those potentialities could be fully developed, some major political anachronisms had to be swept away, as it transpired with rather brutal clarity and far-reaching implications during the crisis.

By the time the crisis erupted in 1929, capital reached the final stages of its transition from "extensive totality" to the relentless exploration and exploitation of the hidden continents of "intensive totality", as a result of the great productive boost it received during the First World War and through the postwar period of reconstruction. While different countries were affected in different ways (depending on capital's relative degree of development and on their status as victors or losers), the new contradictions erupted essentially because the qualitative productive advances of the period could no longer be contained within the historically antiquated power relations of the prevailing "extensive totality".

Marx noticed already in the late 1870s that US capital represented by far the most dynamic force of the global system: a truth which sounded half a century louder in the 1920s. And yet, despite the vital role American capital played in winning the war, the still prevailing political status quo of global domination (established a long time earlier) condemned it to being very much the second fiddle to British imperialism: an anachronism that, obviously, could not be tolerated indefinitely.

Not surprisingly, therefore, the imperative of a new departure had crystallised during the "Great World Crisis". For the devastating pressures of this apparently never ending crisis made it abundantly clear that US capital had to remake the entire world of capital in its own more dynamic image, and that it had no alternative to doing so if it wanted to overcome not merely the immediate critical conditions but also the prospect of chronic depression. Accordingly, beneath the intense rhetorics of Roosevelt's Inaugural Address in 1933 the really significant message was the radically new perspective of *neo-capitalist* colonialism under American hegemony. For it foreshadowed not only Churchill's frustrations during the Second World War as well as the Yalta agreements but—above all—the takeover of the British and French Empires for all intents and purposes, together with the relegation of the historically antiquated varieties of imperialism and colonialism to the second division, where they effectively already belonged, in the higher stakes for the domination of capital's "intensive totality".

Liberal mythology likes to remember Roosevelt as the "man of the people" and as the tireless champion of a "New Deal" for them. In truth, however, his claim to lasting historical fame, even if somewhat dubious, rests on being a far-sighted representative of capital's new-found dynamism, in virtue of his pioneering role both in elaborating the overall strategy and in skillfully laying the practical foundations for neocolonialism.

This meant a two-pronged attack in the framework of a truly *global* orientation. On the one hand, since the imperative of a new departure had arisen on the basis of the great productive advance and the crisis created by its driving to a halt, with respect to its homeward terms of reference the new strategy involved the full exploration of all the hidden continents of "internal colonialism": hence the "New Deal" and the development of an expanding consumer-economy on more secure foundations. At the same time, the need for securing and safeguarding the continued expansion of the home economic base necessarily implied on the other hand the ruthless removal of all the "artificial barriers" of past colonialism (and corresponding protectionist / underdeveloped capitalism).

This neo-capitalist strategy of conquering "intensive totality" was a truly *global* conception also in the sense that it attempted to come to terms with the existence of the Soviet Union, not only for its own sake but also in order to be in a better position to control the emerging anti-colonial movements.

Naturally, all this was supposed to succeed under the unquestionable hegemony of US capital which later went on advertising, with typical vulgarity, its arrogant self-confidence by insisting that the twentieth century was "the American Century". And, of course, in view of the inherent dynamism of the historically most advanced form of capital, the "new world order" (and its "new economic order") was supposed to come into being and remain with us forever through the agency of purely *economic* forces and determinations: so said the rhetorics, from Roosevelt's First Inaugural Address to "the end of ideology".

However, the facts could not speak more differently. For they bitterly put into relief one of the greatest ironies of history, namely: that although an incomparable economic dynamism and a potentially great new productive advance was at the roots of the original Rooseveltian strategy, its actual implementation—far from being satisfied with *economic* mechanisms, in tune with the even today still persisting myth of "modernisation"—required the most devastating war known to man, the Second World War, for its "take-off", not to mention the emergence and domination of the "military-industrial complex" in its real "drive to maturity".

While American capital had much more than simply the initiative in all these developments—indeed it completely dominated them throughout, securing for itself a position of overwhelming advantage through which it can chalk up astronomical budget deficits and make the rest of the world pay for them—they affected and benefited "total social capital" (constituted as a global entity) in its drive for self-expansion and domination.

To be sure, several national constituent parts of the totality of capital had to suffer humiliating immediate defeats, but only so as to rise stronger than ever from the ashes of temporary disability. The German and Japanese "miracles" speak for themselves in this respect. In other cases, notably that of British capital, the impact was much more complicated, for a variety of reasons, concerned mainly with the rearguard struggle over the dissolution of the British Empire. But even in such instances, there can be no denying that in the end a not negligible degree of dynamic restructuring came about under the American challenge.

The overall result of these transformations was a significant *rationalisation of global capital* and the establishment of a framework of financial / economic and state relations which, all in all, was much more suitable for the displacement of many contradictions than the system previously in existence.

2.5

THUS, THE 1929-33 crisis was by no means a structural crisis from the point of view of capital as a global formation. On the contrary, it provided the necessary stimulus and pressure for the realignment of its various constituent forces, in accordance with the objectively changed power relations, greatly contributing thereby to the unfolding of capital's tremendous potentialities as inherent in its "intensive totality".

Externally this meant:

(1) a dramatic move from poly-centred, outdated, wastefully interventionist political / military imperialism to a dynamic, economically much more viable and integrated system of global domination under US hegemony;

(2) the establishment of the International Monetary System and a number of other important organs for the incomparably more rational regulation of inter-capital relations than the poly-centred framework had at its disposal;

(3) the export of capital on a large scale (and through it the most effective perpetuation of dependency and enforced "underdevelopment"), and the secure repatriation, on an astronomical scale, of rates of profit totally unimaginable at home; and

(4) the relative incorporation, to varying degrees, of the economies of all postcapitalist societies into the framework of capitalist interchanges.

Internally, on the other hand, capital's great success story could be described in terms of:

(1) using various modalities of state intervention for the expansion of private capital;

(2) the transfer of bankrupt but essential private industries to the public sector, and their utilisation for supporting through state funds in yet another way the operations of private capital, to be followed in due course by the transformation of such industries into private monopolies or quasi-monopolies, once they have become highly profitable again through the injection of massive funds financed from general taxation;

(3) the successful development and operation of an economy of "full employment" during the war and for a considerable period of time also after the war;

(4) the opening up of new markets and new branches of production on the plane of the highly stretched "consumer-economy", together with capital's success in generating and sustaining extremely wasteful patterns of consumption as a vital motivating force of such an economy; and

(5) to crown it all, both in its sheer economic weight and political significance, the establishment of an immense "military / industrial complex" as the controller and direct beneficiary of by far the most important portion of state intervention, and with it simultaneously also the removal of well over one third of the economy from the unwelcome fluctuations and uncertainties of the market.

Although the intrinsic value of all these achievements is extremely problematical (to put it mildly), there can be no doubt whatsoever as to their significance from the point of view of capital's dynamic self-expansion and continued survival. Precisely because of their central importance in 20th century capitalist developments, the severity of today's structural crisis is heavily underlined by the fact that several of the characteristics mentioned above are no longer true, and that the underlying tendency points in the direction of their reversal altogether: from a trend towards a new poly-centrism (think of Japan and Germany, for instance), with potentially incalculable consequences, to persistent mass unemployment (and its obvious implications for the consumer-economy) as well as to the threatening disintegration of the international monetary system and its corollaries. It would be foolish to take for granted as permanent even the powerfully entrenched positions of the military-industrial complex and its ability to extract and allocate to itself, undisturbed, the surplus required for its continued functioning on the current, still astronomical scale.

SOME PEOPLE argue that since capital managed to solve its problems in the past, it will indefinitely do so also in the future. They might even add that if the crisis of 1929-33 spurred capital to the dramatic changes we have witnessed ever since, the present structural crisis is bound to produce lasting remedies and permanent solutions. The trouble with such reasoning is that it has absolutely nothing to back up the wishful thinking which desperately tries to pursue the "line of least resistance" when it is no longer feasible to do so.

While it is always rather vacuous and dangerous to argue from nothing more than mere analogies of the past, it is self-contradictory to do so when the issue at stake is precisely the structural crisis and breakdown of some, up to now vital, mechanisms and determinations, manifesting itself as the crisis of established control and domination as such. The conditions for a solution of the present crisis can be specified, as we shall see in a moment. Thus, unless it can be demonstrated that capital's contemporary trends of development can actually satisfy these conditions, any talk about its inherent ability to always solve its problems is nothing but "whistling in the dark".

Another line of reasoning insists that capital has at its disposal an immense repressive force which it can freely use, as much as it pleases, for the solution of its mounting problems. Though it is by no means true that there are no constraints— even major ones—on the actual and potential use of naked force by capital, it is unquestionably the case that the already accumulated forces of destruction and repression are frightening, and still multiplying. But even so, the truth remains that nothing is ever solved by force alone, nor has been. Legends to the contrary—concerning Nazism and Stalinism, for instance—are often used merely to explain away a great deal of more or less active complicity of allegedly powerless sections of the population.

In addition, there is a far weightier consideration which concerns the inherent characteristics of capital itself. To put it simply, capital is a most efficient force for mobilising the complex productive resources of a society fragmented in many parts. It does not matter to capital how many: the ability to cope with fragmentation is precisely its great asset. However, capital is definitely not a system of unifying *emergency*, nor could it become one on a long-term basis, for reasons of its own internal constitution. It is by no means accidental in this respect that fascist type state formations are viable today only at the periphery of the global capital system, in dependency and subordination to some liberal-democratic "metropolitan" centre.

Thus, whatever the temporary successes of "iron-fisted" authoritarian attempts might be in delaying or postponing the "moment of truth"—and the chances of even such short-term successes should not be underrated—they can only aggravate the crisis in the longer run. For the structural problems described above amount to a major blockage in the global system of production and distribution. As such, they call for adequate structural remedies, not for their multiplication by forced postponement and repression. In other words, they require a positive intervention in the troubled productive process itself for checking its dangerously growing contradictions, with a view to ultimately removing them as the pace of actual restructuring permits. As against this, to present the possibility of capital resorting, while it can, to rule by way of a completely unstable, hence necessarily *transient*, state of *emergency*, as the *permanent* condition of its future normality, is a truly absurd notion.

2.6

THE CONDITIONS of managing the structural crisis of capital are directly linked to some major contradictions which affect both the internal problems of the various systems involved and their relationships with one another. They may be summed up as follows:

(1) The internal social/economic contradictions of "advanced" capital manifesting in increasingly more lopsided development under the direct or indirect control of the "military-industrial complex" and the system of transnational corporations;

(2) The social, economic and political contradictions of post-capitalist societies, both internally and in relation to one

another, leading to their disintegration and thereby to the intensification of the structural crisis of the global capital system;

(3) The increasing rivalries, tensions and contradictions among the leading capitalist countries, both *within* the various regional systems and *among* them, putting enormous strain on the established institutional framework (from the European Community to the International Monetary System) and foreshadowing the spectre of a devastating trade war;

(4) The growing difficulties of maintaining the established neocolonial system of domination (from Iran to Africa and from South East Asia to Central and Southern America), coupled with the contradictions generated within the "metropolitan" countries through the production units established and managed by "expatriate" capital.

As we can see, in all four categories—each of which stands for a multiplicity of contradictions—the tendency is the intensification, and not the decrease of the existing antagonisms. Furthermore, the severity of the crisis is underlined by effectively confining intervention to the sphere of *effects*, making it prohibitively difficult to tackle their *causes*, thanks to the earlier mentioned "circularity" of capital's civil society/political state through which the established power relations tend to reproduce themselves in all their surface transformations.

Two important examples illustrate this with savage conclusiveness. The first concerns the military-industrial complex, the second the chronic insolubility of the problems of "underdevelopment".

Much hope is expressed about finding the resources for a positive and viable economic expansion through reallocating a major portion of the military expenditure for socially long overdue measures and purposes. However, the permanent frustration of such hopes arises not only from the immense economic weight and naked state power of the military-industrial complex but also from the fact that the latter is more the manifestation and effect of the deep-seated structural contradictions of "advanced" capital than their cause. Naturally, once it exists, it continues to function *also* as a contributory cause— and the greater its economic and political power the more so—but it does not *produce* them in the first place. From the point of view of contemporary capital, if the military-industrial complex did not exist, it ought to have been invented. (As mentioned earlier, in a sense capital simply "stumbled upon" this solution during the war, after Roosevelt's somewhat naive attempt to *reculer pour mieux sauter* from the launching pad of the New Deal, resulting in very little advance indeed in a continued depression rather than in a real jump.)

The military-industrial complex fulfils with great effectiveness two vital functions, displacing temporarily two massive contradictions of "overdeveloped" capital.

The first, mentioned a short while ago, is the transfer of a significant portion of the economy from the treacherous sea of uncontrollable market forces to the sheltered waters of highly profitable state finance. At the same time it also maintains intact also the mythology of economically superior and *cost-effective private enterprise*, thanks to the apriori absolution of *total* wastefulness and *structural bankruptcy* by the ideology of patriotic fervour.

The second function is no less important: to displace the contradictions due to the *decreasing rate of utilisation*[31] which dramatically asserted itself during the last few decades of developments in the capitalistically advanced countries.

This is why, so long as a structural alternative is not found for dealing with the causal foundations of the successfully displaced contradictions here referred to, the hope of simply reallocating the prodigious resources now vested in the military-industrial complex are bound to remain nullified by the prevailing causal determinations.

The same is true of the intractable problems of enforced "underdevelopment". Naturally, it would suit "enlightened capital"—a true contradiction in terms, if ever there was one—to extend its sphere of operation into every pore of "underdeveloped" society, fully activating its material and human resources in the interest of its renewed self-expansion. Hence the efforts of *Brandt Commissions* and similar enterprises which manage to voice a great many partial truths while failing to notice the global one: that the "underdeveloped" world is *already* fully integrated into the world of capital, and fulfils in it a number of vital functions. Thus, again, we can see an attempt to alleviate the *effects* of the dominant mode of integration while leaving their *causal determinations* untouched.

What is systematically ignored in such wishful proposals is that it is quite simply impossible to have it both ways: to maintain "advanced' capital's highly stretched and absurdly "overdeveloped" system of production in existence (which necessarily postulates the continued domination of a vast "hinterland" of enforced underdevelopment) and at the same time to propel the "Third World" to a high level of capitalistic development (which could only reproduce the contradictions of western "advanced" capital, multiplied by the immense size of the population involved).

Capital's managers currently in charge know much better what the real score is—and so did Edward Heath and Willie Brandt themselves, when they were heading their respective governments—and cast aside these reports with the cynical "realism" that directly corresponds to the aggressive reassertion of the dominant US interests:

> United States' Secretary of State said today that it was unrealistic to speak of a big transfer of resources from developed to developing countries. Mr Haig's emphasis was on using conventional market forces [sic!] to alleviate the plight of the poorest countries. There had to be "a more open trading system with improved rules". Foreign assistance had to be coupled with "sound domestic policy and self-help". In the view of the United States that meant relying on economic incentives and individual freedom. "Suppression of economic incentives ultimately suppresses enthusiasm and invention... Those governments that have been more solicitous of the liberties of their people have also been more successful in securing both freedom and prosperity".[32]

To hear a paradigm representative of the repressive military-industrial complex sing the timeless virtues of "conventional market forces" and "individual freedom" is indeed a supreme irony. Sadly, however, it also happens to be a true measure of the utter hopelessness of expecting solutions from improvements in the realm of effects while leaving the causal determinants of capital's real world follow their established course which *structurally* reproduces those effects, with deepening gravity, on an ever-enlarging scale.

If the condition of resolving the structural crisis is tied to the solution of the four sets of contradictions mentioned above, the prospects of a positive outcome are far from promising from the point of view of capital's continued global expansion and domination. For one can see very little chance of success even in regard to relatively limited objectives, let alone in the lasting solution of the contradictions of all four categories combined. The probability is, on the contrary, that we shall continue to sink deeper into the structural crisis, even if there are bound to be some conjunctural successes as well as those resulting from a relative "upturn", in due course, in the merely *cyclic* determinants of capital's present-day crisis.

3.

THE PLURALITY OF CAPITALS AND THE MEANING OF SOCIALIST PLURALISM

3.1

REFLECTING OVER the debates of the Gotha Programme, Engels sarcastically commented on what he considered the deplorable influence of Wilhelm Liebknecht, the main author of the Programme: "From bourgeois democracy he has brought over and maintained a real *mania for unification*".[33] Sixteen years earlier, at the time of the planned Unity Congress, Marx made a similar point about the question of unification, though without the personal references. He acknowledged that "the mere fact of unification is satisfying to the workers", but in the same sentence he stressed that "it is a mistake to believe that this momentary success is not bought at too high a price".[34]

It is important to remember this sceptical attitude towards "unity" and "unification" in order to put in perspective the recent advocacy of pluralism. For it would be quite wrong to treat this problem as something arising either from purely tactical considerations or from the practical constraints of an unfavourable relation of forces which no longer allows the pursuit of consistent socialist policies but calls, instead, for the strategy of elaborate compromises.

Another dimension of this problematic is that for many years the working class movement was subjected to Stalinist-inspired pressures which tried to enforce "unity" so as to automatically suppress criticism in the interest of the "Leading party'. The self-appointed spokesmen of such "unity" never bothered to define the tangible socialist objectives of the advocated organisational *Gleichschaltung* (ie forcing into a set mould), nor indeed to size up the objective conditions of formulating coordinated socialist strategies, together with the immense difficulties of their realisation.

There are some very powerful reasons why Marx and Engels considered "unity" and "unification" as rather problematical concepts: the existing objective divisions and contradictions in the various constituents of the socialist movement. Such divisions and contradictions, in view of their complex internal and international ramifications, could not be simply wished or legislated out of existence; even less so than the eighteenth century French Convention could dream about abolishing pauperism by decree. It was not necessary to wait for the eruption of the Sino-Soviet conflict and the war between China and Vietnam to realise that merely postulating or enunciating the "unity of socialist forces" contributes absolutely nothing to removing their problems, inequalities and antagonisms. The task of developing a force strong enough to successfully challenge capital on its own ground implied from the very beginning the necessity of building on the given foundations which show a great diversity and conflict of interests, as determined by the inherited social division of labour and the long prevailing differential rates of exploitation.

Since the problem was how to constitute a socialist *mass* consciousness on the available foundations while simultaneously engaging in unavoidable confrontations for the realisation of *limited* aims and objectives, it was essential to find ways of preserving the integrity of the *ultimate* perspectives without losing contact with the *immediate* demands, determinations and potentialities of the historically given conditions. For Bakunin and the anarchists this problem did not exist (just as it was of no concern to all subsequent breeds of voluntarism), since they were not interested in the production of a socialist mass consciousness. They simply assumed the spontaneous convergence of the "instinctive conscience of the popular masses" with their own views and strategies.

Marx, by contrast, saw the organisational question as:

(1) remaining faithful to socialist *principles*, and

(2) devising viable and flexible *programmes of action* for the various forces which share the broad common objectives of the struggle. This is how he summed up his views about the Unity Congress in the last quoted letter:

The Lassallean leaders came because circumstances forced them to come. If they had been told in advance that there would be *no bargaining about principles*, they would have had to be content with a *programme of action* or a plan of organisation for common action. Instead of this, one permits them to arrive armed with mandates, recognises these mandates on one's part as valid, and thus *surrenders* unconditionally to those who are themselves in need of help.

Irrespective of the specific circumstances of the Gotha Congress, the "high price" referred to by Marx concerned the compromise of *principles*, in pursuit of an illusory "unity" in place of the feasible and necessary *common action*.

Just as in those days, this happens to be again an issue of paramount importance. For today—perhaps more than ever, in view of the bitter experiences of the recent and not so recent past—the much needed forms of *common action* cannot be conceived without a conscious strategic articulation of a *socialist pluralism* which recognises not only the existing differences but also the need for an adequate "division of labour" in the general framework of a socialist offensive. In opposition to the false identification of "unity" as the only way of championing socialist *principles* (while, in fact, the unrealistic pursuit and imposition of unity carried with it the necessary *compromise of principles*), Marx's rule remains valid: there can be *no bargaining about principles*.

But the obverse side of this rule is equally valid: namely, that the elementary condition of realising the principles of a socialist transformation (which, after all, involves the totality of "associated producers" in the common enterprise of changing "from top to bottom the conditions of their industrial and political existence, and consequently their whole manner of being") is the production of a socialist *mass consciousness* in the only feasible form of self-developing *common action*. And the latter, of course, can only arise out of the truly *autonomous* and *coordinated* (not hierarchically ruled and manipulated) constituents of an *inherently pluralist* movement.

In the socialist movement for a long time it was customary to *underestimate* the ability of the bourgeoisie to achieve unity.

At the same time, there was a corresponding tendency to greatly *overestimate* both the possibilities and the immediate importance of working class unity. Furthermore, the same conceptions which assessed unity so much out of focus with reality also had a tendency to see the conquest of power as the *solution* of the problems confronting the socialist revolution, rather than their *real beginning*.

Naturally, if the socialist revolution is seen as primarily *political* in character, rather than as a multidimensional, and therefore necessarily "permanent" *social* revolution, as Marx defined it, in that case the production and preservation of unity overrides everything in importance. If, however, it is recognised that the acquisition of power is only the *starting point* for unearthing the real difficulties and contradictions of that transformation "from top to bottom, of the whole manner of being" of the associated producers,—difficulties and contradictions many of which cannot be even imagined before actually encountering them in the course of the ongoing transformation itself—then the need for genuinely pluralist strategies asserts itself as a matter of both immediate urgency and continued importance.

In this respect, while it is abstractly true that the ruling class's unity "can only reveal itself vis-à-vis the proletariat,"35 it is also highly misleading. For insofar as everything is subordinated to the fundamental contradiction between capital and labour under capitalism, bourgeois unity inevitably fulfils the function of strengthening one side of this antagonism. The trouble is, though, that the same is true of the other side; and even more so, as we shall see in a moment. Consequently, the abstract truth conceals a misrepresentation of major importance, born from wishful thinking. In other words, it denies or ignores that there is a devastatingly *real* foundation to the ruling class's unity: its *actual* rule and the tangible *power* (both material/economic and political/military) that goes with it.

By contrast, proletarian unity is a problem, a task, a challenge, even an imperative in determinate situations of emergency, but not a spontaneously given actual state of affairs. It may be brought into being for a more or less limited period and for a determinate purpose, but it may never be assumed as an unproblematically persistent condition even after its successful accomplishment in a specific socio-historical situation. On the contrary; it has to be constantly *recreated* under the changing circumstances for as long as the objective grounds of inequality (due to the inherited hierarchical social division of labour and differential rates of exploitation mentioned earlier) remain with us in any form whatsoever, as they are bound to remain for a much longer historical period of transition than one would wish.

3.2

THE "BOURGEOIS mania for unity" referred to by Engels has its solid foundation in the dominant economic order of society and its institutional guarantor, the capitalist state. The political manipulations of formal unity (at times successfully masquerading even as "general consensus") amount to no more than putting the seal of approval on a *de facto* already prevailing state of affairs, thus providing its a *posteriori* "legitimation".

Being effectively in power as a class—and not only politically, thanks to the repressive instrumentality of the state, but in the *positive* sense of regulating the fundamental social metabolism itself—provides a powerful objective ground for a unifying self-identity well before the question of an acute political confrontation with the opposing class may arise. And even as far as the internal divisions of bourgeois "civil society" are concerned, in view of the irrepressible objective tendency of concentration and centralisation of capital the winning side is always the "unitarian" one (ie big capital). The power of the latter multiplies just as certainly as the drive towards monopoly quickens its pace and creates the grotesquely unequal parties to the once idealised but now ever more blatantly predetermined and automatically resolved internal "competition". Hence the ever-increasing *sham pluralism* of the social order of capital in all its contemporary permutations.

One of the most powerful political/ideological mystifications of capital is, in fact, its pretence to "pluralism" through which it succeeds in ruthlessly prescribing the framework of all admissible opposition to its own rule. While at the liberal/democratic phase of capitalist developments the claim to pluralism still meant something (even if not much more than the possibilities inherent in John Stuart Mill's "negative freedom"), ever since the onset of the *monopolistic* phase the margin of real alternatives has been getting narrower and narrower, to the point of its almost complete disappearance in recent times. If the monetarist nightmare today finds its crude, inarticulate articulation in TINA ("there is no alternative", as Ministers carry on repeating, like a broken gramophone record, the cynical message of capital's real freedom), that can only underline the gravity of the structural crisis. Besides, it also underlines the difficulties of a continued misrepresentation of the *absolute tyranny* of capital's economic determinism as "the greatest good of the greatest number" and the apotheosis of "traditional market forces and individual freedom".

In truth, right from the beginning "pluralism" was an extremely problematical concept for capital. Not only—and not even primarily—because of its *tendency* towards monopoly, but because of the *absolute presupposition* of monopoly as its *starting point*: ie the monopoly of private property by the few and the apriori exclusion of the vast majority as the necessary prerequisite of capital's social control. (It is worth mentioning here that state-monopoly of the means of production retains this vital presupposition of the capital system and thereby perpetuates the rule of capital under a different form.) All subsequent rules of capital's "pluralist" game were decreed on this absolute monopolistic foundation: in its own interest, and to be broken in the interest of its continued rule, whenever the circumstances so required.

It was assumed as self-evident right from the beginning that "there can be no alternative" to the monopoly of the means of production, nor to the free reign of capital's steamrolling economic determinism. If someone—followers of Marx, for instance—dared to question the destructive manifestations and implications of such economic determinism, they had to be condemned as dangerous "economic determinists" from the standpoint of capital's one-dimensional and uni-directional freedom. The meaning of capital's "pluralism" never amounted to more than simply acknowledging the *plurality of capitals* while simultaneously also insisting on total capital's absolute right to *monopoly*, both *tendentially* and *de facto*.

Thus, not only there can be no affinity between socialist pluralism and capitalist pseudo-pluralism (which does not and cannot offer a bigger margin of alternative action than is required by the narrow self-interest of a plurality of competing capitals, and even that only so long as their limited competition remains viable); they are, in fact, diametrically opposed to one another.

The meaning of capital's pluralism is visible at the political level in the farcical ritual of "competing" for power between Democrats and Republicans in the US, just as much as in the successful manipulation of political power on behalf of capital by one wretched party in Italy, the Christian Democrats, for well over four decades and a half without interruption. (That the rule of Japanese capital is effectively linked to a curious one-party system, cleverly exploiting the traditional allegiances of a paternalistic society, is obvious even to its capitalist critics.) And in the somewhat more complicated cases of England and Germany (where Social Democracy openly boasted about its ability to better administer a "modern" capitalist "mixed economy" than the conservative alternative, self-delusorily trying to legitimate its claim to being "the natural party of government" on such a noble foundation), only the form of "pluralist" mystification is different, not its substance. This is why the conservative Edward Heath and the social democratic Willy Brandt end up on the same side in a tame critique of the system when *both* their parties happen to be in government. And this is why Willy Brandt's successor, Helmut Schmidt, can only conceptualise (and denounce) the possibility of a socialist challenge to capital's rule as "political destabilisation".

In all these cases "pluralism" means a *systematic political disenfranchising* of labour in its confrontation with capital, in the form most appropriate to the local circumstances. The "pluralism" of changing governments (how many of them in postwar Italy, without the slightest change at all?) provides the *permanent alibi* for categorically rejecting any real change and for cynically enforcing the imperative according to which "there can be no alternative" to capital's devastating economic determinism. Furthermore, the institutions of capital's pseudo-pluralism not only provide the immediate political guarantees of its continued rule. They also act as a mystifying shield that automatically diverts all criticism from its real target (namely the vicious circle of capital's destructive self-expansion to which everything must be unquestioningly subordinated) to the personalised irrelevance of its willing administrators who fall over backwards in outbidding one another as to who can keep the mechanism of the system better oiled.

Thus, the possibility of "consensual" change is conveniently relegated to a margin of action apriori set by the premise that "there is no alternative" to the requirements of capital's self-expansion (no matter how destructive), successfully enforcing thereby the dictates of the narrowest kind of economic determinism as the ultimate fulfillment of freedom. For the diversionary target of consensual political opposition makes it sure that whenever governments are booted out of office by bitterly disillusioned "sovereign" electorates for "breaking their promises", the awesome responsibility and dubious viability of the social/economic order which they serve and on whose behalf they make and break those promises is never even mentioned. Accordingly, while "pluralist" governments may come and go with mystifying frequency, the rule of capital remains absolutely intact.

3.3

IN COMPLETE contrast, the elementary condition of success of the socialist project is its inherent pluralism. It sets out from the acknowledgement of the existing differences and inequalities; not to preserve them (which is a necessary concomitant of all fictitious and arbitrarily enforced "unity") but to supersede them in the only viable form: by securing the active involvement of all those concerned.

The latter, it goes without saying, is impossible without the elaboration of specific strategies and "mediations", arising from the particular determinations of changing needs and circumstances, which represent the greatest challenge to contemporary Marxist theory. For the one and only broadly held view that can serve as a common framework of reference for the great variety of politically more or less organised and conscious socialist forces is the *rejection* of the ubiquitous

slogan that "there is no alternative". And even that cannot be
assumed as unproblematically given. Not only because it is a
negativity which needs its positive articulation in order to
become viable as a mobilising strategy, but also because in the
first instance it amounts to no more than merely asserting that
"there *ought to be* an alternative". However, it remains the necessary starting point. For those who accept the wisdom of
"there is no alternative"—in the name of the "triumph of
organised capitalism", or the "integration of the working
class", or whatever else—could hardly claim *also* to offer the
perspective of a socialist transformation, even if sometimes,
curiously, they continue to do so.

Just as capital is structurally incapable of pluralism (other
than one of a very limited kind, and even that becoming more
and more restricted with the advance of capital's necessary
concentration and centralisation), so the socialist enterprise is
structurally unrealisable without its full articulation in the manifold autonomous ("self-managing"), and thus irrepressibly
pluralist projects of the ongoing *social revolution*.

The broad general principle rejecting capital's economic
determinism provides no more than a necessary point of
departure in relation to which all particular groups (inevitably
reflecting a multiplicity of given interests and divisions) must
define their position in the form of interconnected, and if conditions permit also coordinated, but definitely not identical
specific objectives and strategies. What is at stake is to devise a
viable alternative to an immensely complex global system
which has on its side the "curse of interdependence" in resist-
ing change.

This is expressed with brutal clarity in the words of Sir Roy
Denman, EEC's chief negotiator for many years on international trade relations:

> *There is no alternative.* People are not *insane* enough to
> want a *massive unravelling of the whole system.* Yet the dan-
> gers are very great, the situation is more serious now
> than at any time since the last war.[36]

Thus, the spokesmen of capital, even when they are forced
to acknowledge the severity of the crisis, can find reassurance

in the prevailing "sanity" that protects and imposes the system as the one to which "there is no alternative". And even though it cannot be all that reassuring to be left with nothing more solid than the ultimate *fiat* of "sanity" in defence of capitalist insanity, it remains true that a *massive unravelling of the whole system* is the only real alternative to capital's deepening structural crisis.

No one can seriously suggest that Sir Roy Denman's "insanity"—the "massive unravelling of the whole system" and its replacement by a viable one—could be accomplished by small groups of fragmented, isolated people. In reality, there can be no escape from Marx's programme of constituting a socialist mass consciousness through the practical enterprise of engaging in actually feasible and inherently pluralist common action.

While it becomes painfully obvious that capital's alternatives today are more and more confined to manipulative fluctuations between varieties of *Keynesianism* and *monetarism*,[37] with perilously less and less effective oscillatory movements tending toward the "absolute rest" of a depressed continuum, the socialist rejection of the tyranny of "no alternative" must be positively articulated in the form of intermediary objectives whose realisation can make strategic inroads, even if in the first instance only partial ones, into the system to be replaced.

WHAT DECIDES the fate of the various socialist forces in their confrontation with capital is the extent to which they can make tangible changes in everyday life now dominated by the ubiquitous manifestations of the underlying contradictions. Thus, it is not enough to focus on the structural determinants—even if it is done with insight, from an adequate vantage point—if at the same time their directly felt manifestations are left out of sight, because their socialist strategic implications are not visible to those concerned. For the meaning of socialist pluralism—the active engagement in common action, without compromising but constantly renewing the socialist principles which inspire the overall concerns—arises precisely from the ability of the participating forces to *combine* into a coherent whole, with *ultimately* inescapable socialist implications, a great variety of demands and partial strategies which in and by themselves need not have anything *specifically socialist* about them at all.

In this sense, the most urgent demands of our times, directly corresponding to the vital needs of a great variety of social groups—for jobs and education as well as for a decent health care and social services, together with the demands inherent in the struggle for women's liberation and against racial discrimination—are, without one single exception, such that, in principle, every genuine liberal could wholeheartedly embrace them. It is rather different, though, when we consider them not as single issues, in isolation, but jointly, as parts of the overall complex that constantly reproduces them as unrealised and systematically unrealisable demands.

Thus, it is the *condition* of their realisation that ultimately decides the issue, (defining them in their plurality as *conjointly* socialist demands) and not their character considered separately. Consequently, what is at stake is not the elusive "politicisation" of these separate concerns through which they might in the end fulfil a direct political function in a socialist strategy, but the *effectiveness* of asserting and sustaining such largely self-motivating "non-socialist" demands on the broadest possible front.

The immediate concerns of everyday life, from health care to grain production, are not directly translatable into the general values and principles of a social system. (Even comparisons become relevant and effective only when there is a shortfall in one area as a result of the more or less unjustifiable demands of another; like today's cuts in vital social services in the interest of the war-industry.) Any attempt at imposing a direct political control on such movements, following the rather unhappy tradition of the not so distant past, is in danger of being counterproductive (even if for the best intentions of "politicisation"), instead of helping to strengthen their autonomy and effectiveness.

It is an important sign of the historically changed conditions that these demands and the forces behind them can no longer be "incorporated" or "integrated" into capital's objective dynamics of self-expansion. In view of their chronic insolubility, as well as their immediate motivating power, they are likely to set the framework of social confrontation for the foreseeable future. Naturally, no matter how important even on their own, the issues referred to above were mentioned here only as *examples* belonging to a much larger number of specific concerns through which socialist aspirations and strategies must mediate themselves today.

Another type of demand involves a more obvious and direct social/political commitment, although even this set cannot be characterised as specifically socialist. For instance, the intensifying struggle for preserving peace against the vested interests of the military-industrial complex, or the need for curbing the power of the transnationals, or indeed for establishing a basis of cooperation and interchange in order to secure the conditions of real development in the "Third World". While it is fairly obvious that capital cannot meet any of these demands, and thus its control over the forces behind them is diminishing, it is also true that the liberating potential of its slipping control cannot be realised without the articulation of adequate socialist strategies and corresponding organisational forms.

The demands that directly manifest the necessity of a socialist alternative concern the inherent wastefulness of capital's mode of functioning. For, paradoxically, capital manages to impose on society the "iron law" of its *economic determinism* without knowing the meaning of *economy* at all. There are four main directions in which the necessary wastefulness of capital asserts itself with increasingly more harmful consequences, as the ultimate limits of its productive potential are approached:

(1) the uncontrollable demand for *resources*—ie capital's irrepressibly rising "resource-intensity", of which "energy-intensity" is only one aspect—irrespective of the consequences for the future, or for the environment, or indeed for repressing the needs of the people afflicted by its so-called "developmental strategies";

(2) the growing *capital-intensity* of its production processes, inherent in the necessary concentration and centralisation of capital, and greatly contributing to the production of "underdevelopment" not only on the "periphery" but even in the heartland of its "metropolitan" domain, generating massive unemployment and devastating a once flourishing and in many respects perfectly viable industrial base;

(3) the accelerating drive for the *multiplication of exchange-value*, at first simply *divorced* from but now more and more openly *opposed* to "use-value" in the service of *human need*, for the sake of maintaining capital's rule over society intact; and

(4) the worst kind of waste: the waste of people, through the mass production of *"superfluous people"* who, both as a result of capital's "productive" advances and its increasing difficulties in the "realisation process", cannot fit any longer into the narrow schemes of the production of profit and the wasteful multiplication of exchange-value. (The fact that the mass-produced "superfluous time" of the growing number of "superfluous people" is the once only given life-time of real people, cannot be, of course, of any concern to capital's devoted personifications.)

3.4

IN RELATION to all these tendencies and contradictions of capital, demands for a change can only be formulated in terms of a global socialist alternative. It is in this respect that the renewal of Marxism is so vital. For despite the criticisms concerning the "crisis of Marxism", there is no serious alternative theory anywhere in sight which might be able to address itself to these problems in their complexity and comprehensiveness.

Apart from the recent hostile critics of Marx (like the "new French philosophers" and their "post-modernist" stable-mates) who may be safely ignored on account of their all too obvious ideological interests and corresponding intellectual standard, the various critical reflections tend to focus on limited aspects of the current social crisis. They offer answers and solutions which are applicable only partially, and avoid precisely those comprehensive issues which define the strategic horizons of any viable alternative.

While it is necessary to resist the inclination of some Marxists to dismiss this type of criticism as "populist"—for, surely, there must be an important place for socialist inspired "populism" in a genuinely pluralist framework of common action—the concern with local issues and "grass root" forms of organisation, as well as with the task of understanding their historical traditions and "peculiarities", is far from sufficient on its own. It must be complemented by tackling their much broader ramifications and links with the social totality, so that their cumulative impact strengthens the chances of socialist strategy, instead of pulling in the direction of fragmentation and dispersal.

If in the past Marxist theory had a tendency to neglect such concerns, preferring to concentrate on the general principles of the socialist alternative, that was to a significant extent due to the historically *defensive* conditions. So long as such conditions prevailed, the repeated reassertion of the *ultimate* validity of the overall perspectives—in a defiant dismissal of capital's untroubled self-expansion as ultimately irrelevant—was understandable, indeed necessary, even if problematical. Under the changed conditions of the necessary *offensive*, however, the self-reassuring restatement of the general perspectives in the abstract—as a declaration of faith—is completely out of place. For Marx's dictum about *"hic Rhodus, hic salta"* calls for integrating the totality of social demands, from the most immediate "non-socialist" everyday concerns to those openly questioning capital's social order as such, into a theoretically coherent as well as instrumentally / organisationally viable strategic alternative.

Thus, the real issue is how to set firmly an overall direction to follow while fully acknowledging the constraining circumstances and the power of immediacy opposed to ideal shortcuts. The Marxian social revolution defines the period of transition in terms of identifiable objectives, together with the theoretical, material and instrumental mediations necessary for their realisation. In this sense, to name a few vital issues, the question that must be pursued is: how is it possible

(1) to produce a *radical change* while safeguarding the necessary *continuity* of the social metabolism (which calls for the sustained practical application of the Marxian methodological principle concerning the dialectical reciprocity between continuity and change);

(2) to restructure "from top to bottom" the *whole* edifice of society which simply cannot be pulled down for the purposes of a total reconstruction;

(3) to move from the prevailing *fragmentation* of the social forces to their cohesion in the creative enterprise of the *associated producers* (which implies the successful development of socialist *mass consciousness* through assuming *responsibility* for the consequences of self-managed productive and distributive practices);

(4) to accomplish a genuine *autonomy* and *decentralisation* of the powers of decision making, in opposition to their existing

concentration and centralisation which cannot possibly function without "bureaucracy";

(5) to transcend the division and "circular inertia" of *civil society/political state* through the unification of the functions of *work* and *decision making*;

(6) to abolish the everywhere prevailing *secrecy* of government by instituting a new form of *open self-government* by the people concerned.

Many important themes of twentieth century Marxist theory are integral parts of tackling these issues of transition, just as the question of reassessing the role of trade unions and parties in the framework of socialist pluralism has been brought to the forefront again. Some may wish to deny that such issues are important today. But those who do not take that view should not find it difficult to agree that actively engaging with them may well be the most fruitful way of tackling the "crisis of Marxism".

4.

THE NEED TO COUNTER CAPITAL'S
EXTRA-PARLIAMENTARY FORCE

4.1

WE LIVE in an age when—due to the internal dynamics of "hybridisation" of the established mode of social metabolic control—the *political* dimension is much more prominent than in the classical phase of capital's historical ascendancy, despite all protestations of the "radical right" to the contrary.

Naturally, the proper assessment of this problem should not be restricted to the direct political institutions, like parliament. It is much broader and more deep-seated than that. In fact the changes which we have witnessed in the functioning of parliament itself—changes tending to deprive it even of its limited autonomous functions of the past—cannot be circularly explained in terms of the changing electoral machinery and the corresponding parliamentary practices. Spokesmen and women of the hypostatised "absolute sovereignty of parliament" and their rhetorical clashes with their parliamentary colleagues over the mirage of "losing sovereignty to Brussels" (for instance), are wide off the mark. They seek remedies to the deplored changes where they cannot be found: within the confines of the parliamentary political domain itself.

The problem is, though, that the ongoing, and from a self-referential political perspective utterly bewildering, developments can only be understood in the comprehensive framework of the material and cultural reproduction process. For it is the latter that requires the fulfillment of determinate but changing functions from the political sphere in the course of the historical transformations and self-assertive adjustments of the dominant social metabolic order as a whole.

As we have seen above in various contexts, 20th century

developments were characterised by the growing weight of "extra-economic" factors. In other words, the 20th century has witnessed the rise to prominence of "extra-economic" forces and procedures which used to be considered with great scepticism, and rejected as alien to the nature of the capital system at the time of its triumphal historical ascendancy. When with the onset of the structural crisis of the system, in the 1970s, the representatives of the "radical right" broke with the Keynesian form of consensual capitalist state intervention (dominant for a quarter of a century after the Second World War), many of the politicians involved instantly forgot not only that they themselves were deeply implicated in the sinful practices which they now sonorously denounced. They blinded themselves also to the fact—and it is unimportant here whether with the help of hypocrisy and cynical pretence or out of genuine ignorance—that the altered course of action required at least as great a state intervention in the socioeconomic processes (now more than ever on behalf of big business) as the Keynesian variety beforehand. The only difference was that, in addition to the generous help given to big business—from massive tax incentives to corrupt "privatisation" practices,38 and from abundant research funds (especially for the benefit of the military/industrial complex) to the more or less open facilitation of the tendency to monopolism—the "radical right" had to impose also a whole range of repressive laws on the labour movement. Ironically, the repressive laws against labour had to be introduced "softly softly" through the good offices of "democratic parliaments", in order to deny to the working classes even the defensive gains of the past, in accordance with the narrowing margins of profitable capital-accumulation under the circumstances of the unfolding structural crisis.

Thus the importance of political struggle and the radical critique of the state—including its "democratic institutions", with parliament at their apex—has never been greater for the prospects of labour's emancipation than in the present historical phase of the pretended "rolling back the boundaries of the state". As it has become painfully obvious through the worsening plight of billions of people, the capital system—even in its most advanced form—has miserably failed humankind. The same can be said of its political dimension of social metabolic control. For even the most advanced state form of the capital system—the liberal-democratic state, with its parliamentary representation and institutionalised formal democratic guarantees for "justice and fairness", together with its alleged safeguards against the abuse of power—has failed to deliver any of its claimed self-legitimating promises.

The crisis of politics all over the world, including the parliamentary democracies in the capitalistically advanced countries—often assuming the form of understandable bitterness and a resigned withdrawal from political activity by the popular masses—is an integral part of the deepening structural crisis of the capital system. The claims of "empowering the people"—be that under the ideology of "people's capitalism" (armed with a handful of non-voting shares) or under the slogans of "equal opportunity" and "fairness" in a system of incorrigible structural inequality—are too absurd to be taken seriously even by its prominent propagandists. The future is, on the contrary, likely to bring ever greater imposition of regressive political determinations over the everyday life of the popular masses, rather than the repeatedly promised "rolling back the boundaries of the state". There can be no way of opting out of politics, no matter how disheartening its dominant institutional forms and their self-perpetuating practices. But precisely for that reason, politics is too important to be left to politicians; and, indeed, democracy worthy of its name is far too important to be left to capital's actually existing and feasible parliamentary democracies and to the corresponding narrow margin of action of parliamentarians; even of "great parliamentarians".

When the title of "great parliamentarian" is conferred upon representatives of the Left, it is used by the conservative system (with a small "c", including the Labour party's right wing leadership) as a way of congratulating and patting itself on the back. Such political figures are supposed to be "great parliamentarians" because, as the legend goes, they have "learned to master the rules of parliamentary procedure" and with their help "continue to raise uncomfortable issues". However, the truly uncomfortable truth is that the issues thus raised are invariably ignored, or ruled "out of order" in parliament itself. In this way the apologists of the substantively anti-socialist parliamentary system can demonstrate to "demo-

cratic public opinion" that there can be no other way of dealing with the problems of society than submission to the rules
of the parliamentary game and the strict observance of its procedures which produce "great parliamentarians" also on the
political Left. *Futility* and *political marginalisation* are the criteria for being promoted to the exalted rank of "great
parliamentarians" on the Left. Thus a few of them are allowed
into the hall of fame in the interest of putting the system of
parliamentary democracy beyond and above all conceivable
"legitimate criticism".

In truth, given the political marginalisation inseparable from
the acceptance of parliamentary constraints as the only legitimate framework of political action, conformity to the
internalised rules of the parliamentary game—even if it is prac-
tised with radical intent—can only produce the *parliamentary
self-imprisonment* of the Left. Ironically, the way the parliamentary system actually functions, now even people with
impeccable right-wing credentials—but great illusions about
their own role in determining the outcome of political
debates—like Roy Hattersley, are unhappy about the blind con-
formism with which they have to accept the latest rules of the
parliamentary game. They have to complain, of course totally
in vain, that the party leadership should pay more attention to
its once professed principles. In fact we witness today the liqui-
dation of even the mildest social democratic principles in the
name of securing a "broad electoral alliance". Revealingly, thus,
Hattersly is arguing—in an article published in the *Independent*
on 12 August 1995 under the title: "Roy Hattersley tells Tony
Blair where he has gone wrong"—that

> I am a passionate believer in New Labour, a long time
> opponent of old Clause IV [the clause promising the
> common ownership of the means of production] and a
> heretic who wants completely to sever Labour's formal
> links with the trade unions. But I nevertheless understand
> why party members worry that we have become so pre-
> occupied with the problems of the middle classes that we
> have begun to overlook the needs of the disadvantaged
> and the dispossessed... Ideology is what keeps parties
> consistent and credible as well as honest. In the long term,

the party's public esteem would be protected by a robust statement of fundamental intention. Socialism—which is proclaimed in New Clause IV—requires the bedrock of principle to be the redistribution of power and wealth. If that objective were reasserted, many of the problems would disappear.

The fact that the Labour party—of which not so long ago Roy Hattersley was the deputy leader—failed to "redistribute power and wealth" throughout its long history, does not seem to worry the author of this article. The *Times* leader is much more realistic when it sings the praises of Tony Blair, saying that "The 'New Labour' ideology championed by the Opposition leader bears little relation to the socialism of the past. It is *pragmatic, friendly to business*".[39]

4.2

THE NARROWING margin of profitable capital-accumulation greatly affected the prospects of the labour movement even in the capitalistically most advanced countries. For it not only worsened the standard of living of the labour force in full employment (not to mention the conditions of countless millions of unemployed and underemployed people), but, as mentioned in the last section, also curtailed the possibilities of their self-defensive action as a result of authoritarian legislation imposed on the working classes by their allegedly democratic parliaments.

As of today, this process is by no means completed. There is no year in which the working classes are not confronted by new legislative measures devised against their traditional defensive organs and forms of action. At the same time the parliamentary form of representation itself has become extremely problematical even in its own terms of reference.

Once upon a time the justification for the relative autonomy of parliamentary representatives—an argument still used for rationalising the non-accountability of parliamentary representatives to their electors—was summed up in these terms by Hegel:

their relation to their electors is not that of agents with a commission or specific instructions. A further bar to their being so is the fact that their assembly is *meant to be a living body in which all members deliberate in common and reciprocally instruct and convince each other.*[40]

In the actual functioning of parliaments nothing corresponds today to the Hegelian characterisation even to the limited extent to which they could be once described in such terms. Whatever might be the views held by the particular members of parliament on which they would like to "deliberate in common and reciprocally instruct and convince each other", the arguments they might be able to master in favour of their views, even if strongly held, carry no weight. For as a matter of fact the so-called "three line whip" compels them to vote according to the dictates of their party leadership, on pain of "losing their whip" as a result of which they are subsequently "deselected" as parliamentary candidates. This practice is followed not only in dealing with major political issues but even on debates about the desirability of introducing dog licences. There is no difference in this respect between the major political parties. "Left of centre" Labour prime minister Harold Wilson once threatened, with brutal authoritarianism, his dissenting colleagues on the left of the party by saying to them that unless they behaved he would not *"renew their dog licences"*.

This is a most challenging problem for the future. For in the course of this century we have witnessed the degradation of parliamentary politics—once rooted in the plurality of capitals and in the margin of relative gains that could be derived from the corresponding divergence of interests also to limited sections of the working class—to some sort of a *conspiracy* against labour as the antagonist of capital. This kind of conspiracy takes place not so much *between* parties but *within* each of them. Between them only in the sense that the unholy "consensus politics" of these decades—despite the institutionalised fog-generation of parliamentary "adversarial politics"—also belongs to this issue. However, the most important aspect is the internal constitution and functioning of the parties themselves, including the parliamentary parties of labour. For the way they are constituted and run excludes any possibility of even raising the question of how to alter the established mode of social metabolic control. On the contrary, all parliamentary political activity is confined—both in government and in opposition—to the stabilisation or re-stabilisation of the capital system. This is why now for a long time the guiding thread of parliamentary politics has been how to *disenfranchise* labour (not openly and formally but in substantive terms), so as to nullify its gains obtained through the instrumentality of the early working class parties and trade unions. The policy somersaults of the British Labour party (now respectfully calling itself "New Labour"), and the similar "disengagement" of the Italian Communist party from all of its former principles and beliefs, are good illustrations of the way in which the antagonist of capital has been effectively disenfranchised in the course of these developments.

The principal role of social democratic parties (under a variety of names, including those of the rebaptised former Communist parties) is nowadays confined to *delivering labour to capital*, and using the people as *electoral fodder* for the purposes of the spurious legitimation of the perpetuated status quo under the pretext of the "open" and "fully democratic" electoral process. This uncritical parliamentary accommodation of working class parties was by no means always the case, even though the "strict observance of parliamentary procedures" to which they were expected to submit when they entered the electoral arena was always extremely problematical. For the labour movement, at the time of its inception, had much broader and incomparably more radical objectives than what could be realised within the framework of the principal political organ created by the bourgeoisie in the ascendant: Parliament. Indeed, even the German social democratic movement—which started to yield to accommodatory pressures already in Marx's lifetime—continued to promise a radical social transformation through the implementation of strategic reforms until it openly capitulated to the requirements of bourgeois national expansionism at the outbreak of the First World War. Now, however, with the end of capital's historical ascendancy, the margin of even the most limited reform in favour of labour is practically non-existent. Thus the mainstream of "reform" and parliamentary legislation has for its objective the castration of the labour movement in general, and not just the total isolation of the handful of its committed socialist parliamentarians.

Every single institution of the system is fully involved in this enterprise, notwithstanding the mythology of "democratic guarantees" which are supposed to be provided by the "division of powers": a mythology that infected even some well known intellectuals on the left. What is supposed to be one of the principal democratic guarantees—the "fearlessly independent judiciary"—continues to demonstrate on every possible occasion its "independent" ability to extend the repressive laws of "democratic parliament" against labour fully in tune with the interests and imperatives of the established order. Its behaviour during the one year long miners' strike provided striking examples of "judiciary militancy". But, of course, the judiciary does not need a major social confrontation, like the miners' strike, to fulfil its class conscious anti-democratic role. It does so as a matter of normality on every key issue. Thus a recent—and in domestic law final—judgement by the British law lords attacks the trade unions even in their basic wage-negotiating function, undermining thereby their very existence. As reported in the *Financial Times*:

> The law lords unanimously ruled yesterday that employers were legally entitled to withhold pay rises from employees who refused to sign personal contracts that removed their union-based negotiating rights.[41]

This transparently class-conscious judgement was in fact a retrospective extension of a 1993 anti-union law by the Conservative government in Britain, although procedures of this kind are usually misrepresented, with characteristic hypocrisy, as "politically independent legal clarification". What beats, however, even the hypocrisy of such anti-democratic acts is the "reasoning" in which they are wrapped up in order to make them appeal to the credulity of those who are credulous enough to take them seriously. Thus:

> Lord Slynn argued there was no evidence that withholding a salary increase from those who remained in the union was meant to prevent or deter union membership,

even if *derecognition* in itself might make the union less attractive to members or potential members.[42]

There can be no doubt about the mental gymnastics and acrobatics at work in producing rationalisations like this, which call for the unique ability to stand on one's head for the duration of writing lengthy supreme court judgements without even blushing. At the same time, such acts of the highest independent democratic judiciary also confirm with eloquence that the *"separation of powers"* under the rule of capital can only mean one thing: the *institutionalised and legally enforced separation of power from labour and its exercise against the interests of labour.* This is why there can be no hope for instituting meaningful structural changes even in a million years within the confines of the established and well entrenched sociopolitical framework. The permanent frustrations and invariable defeats of genuine socialists who hoped to achieve their objectives now for well over a century through parliamentary reforms were and remain unavoidable precisely for this reason. Their far from simply personal failures underline the wisdom of the great Hungarian poet, Attila József, who wrote:

> *even the best tricks of cat won't catch the mouse*
> *at the same time outside and inside the house.*[43]

4.3

THE CRITIQUE of the parliamentary system from a radical perspective did not begin with Marx. We find it powerfully expressed already in the 18th century in Rousseau's writings. Starting from the position that sovereignty belongs to the people and therefore it cannot be rightfully alienated, Rousseau also argued that for the same reasons it cannot be legitimately turned into any form of representational abdication:

> The deputies of the people, therefore, are not and cannot be its representatives; they are merely its stewards, and can carry through no definitive acts. Every law the people has not ratified in person is null and void—is, in fact, not a

law. The people of England regards itself as free; but it is grossly mistaken; it is free only during the election of members of parliament. As soon as they are elected, slavery overtakes it, and it is nothing. The use it makes of the short moments of liberty it enjoys shows indeed that it deserves to lose them.[44]

At the same time Rousseau also made the important point that although the power of legislation cannot be divorced from the people even through parliamentary representation, the administrative or "executive" functions must be considered in a very different light. As he had put it:

> in the exercise of the legislative power, the people cannot be represented; but in that of the executive power, which is only the force that is applied to give the law effect, it both can and should be represented.[45]

In this way Rousseau, who has been systematically misrepresented and abused by "democratic" ideologues even of the "socialist jet-set" because he insisted that *"liberty cannot exist without equality"*[46]—which therefore ruled out even the best feasible form of representation as necessarily discriminatory/iniquitous hierarchy—had put forward a much more practicable exercise of political and administrative power than what he is usually credited with or indeed is accused of doing. Significantly, in this process of tendentious misrepresentation, both of the vitally important principles of Rousseau's theory, usable in a suitably adapted form also by socialists, have been disqualified and thrown overboard. Yet the truth of the matter is that, on the one hand, the power of fundamental decision making should never be divorced from the popular masses, as the veritable horror story of the Soviet state system, run against the people by the Stalinist bureaucracy in the name of socialism in the most authoritarian fashion, conclusively demonstrated it. At the same time, on the other hand, the fulfillment of specific administrative and executive functions in all domains of the social reproductive process can indeed be *delegated* to members of the given community, provided that it is done under rules autonomously set by and properly controlled at all stages of the substantive decision making process by the associated producers.

Thus the difficulties do not reside in the two basic principles themselves as formulated by Rousseau but in the way in which they must be related to capital's material and political control of the social metabolic process. For the establishment of a socialist form of decision making, in accordance with the principles of both inalienable rule-determining power (ie the "sovereignty" of labour not as a particular class but as the universal condition of society) and delegating specific roles and functions under well defined, flexibly distributed and appropriately supervised, rules would require entering and radically restructuring capital's antagonistic material domains. A process which would have to go well beyond what could be successfully regulated by considerations derived from Rousseau's principle of inalienable popular sovereignty and its delegatory corollary. In other words, in a socialist order the "legislative" process would have to be fused with the production process itself in such a way that the necessary *horizontal division of labour*—discussed in Chapter 14 of *Beyond Capital*—should be complemented by a system of self-determined *co-ordination* of labour, from the local to the global levels. This relationship is in sharp contrast to capital's pernicious *vertical division of labour* which is complemented by the "separation of powers" in an alienated and on the labouring masses unalterably superimposed "democratic political system". For the vertical division of labour under the rule of capital necessarily affects and incurably infects every facet also of the horizontal division of labour, from the simplest productive functions to the most complicated balancing processes of the legislative jungle. The latter is an ever denser legislative jungle not only because its endlessly multiplying rules and institutional constituents must play their vital part in keeping firmly under control the actually or potentially challenging behaviour of labour, watchful over limited labour disputes as well as safeguarding capital's overall rule in society at large. Also, they must somehow reconcile at any particular temporal slice of the unfolding historical process—to the extent to which such reconciliation is feasible at all—the separate interests of the plurality of capitals with the uncontrollable dynamics of the totality of social capital tending towards its ultimate self-assertion as a global entity.

In a recent rejoinder with Rousseau's critique of parliamentary representation, Hugo Chávez Frias, the leader of a radical movement in Venezuela—the Movimiento Bolivariano Revolucionário (MBR-200)—writes in response to the chronic crisis of the country's sociopolitical system:

> With the appearance of the populist parties the suffrage was converted into a tool for putting to sleep in order to enslave the Venezuelan people in the name of democracy. For decades the populist parties based their discourse on innumerable paternalistic promises devised to melt away popular consciousness. The alienating political lies painted the "promised land" to be reached via a rose garden. The only thing the Venezuelans had to do was to go to the electoral urns, and hope that everything will be solved without the minimal popular effort... Thus the act of vote was transformed into the beginning and the end of democracy.[47]

The author of these lines stands the second highest in popular esteem in Venezuela (second only to Rafael Caldera) among all public figures, embracing all walks of life, way above all aspiring party politicians. Thus he could easily win high public office if he so wanted, which refutes the usual argument that people who criticise the existing political system only do so because they are unable to meet the arduous requirements of democratic elections. As a matter of fact Hugo Chávez at the time of writing (in 1993) rejects the "siren song" of political opinion formers—who try to pacify people by saying that there is no need to worry about the crisis because there is "only a little time" to go to the new elections—for very different reasons. He points out that while the usual political advice calls for "a little more patience" until the election scheduled a few months ahead, "every minute hundreds of children are born in Venezuela whose health is endangered for lack of food and medicine, while billions are stolen from the national wealth, and in the end what remains of the country is bled dry. There is no reason why one should give any credence to a political class which demonstrated towards society that it has no will at all to institute change".[48] For this reason Chávez counterposes to the existing system of parliamentary representation the idea that "the sovereign people must transform itself into the object *and the subject* of power. This option is not negotiable for revolutionaries".[49] As to the institutional framework in which this principle should be realised, he projects that in the course of radical change

> Federal state electoral power will become the political-juridical component through which the citizens will be depositories of popular sovereignty whose exercise will thereafter really remain in the hands of the people. Electoral power will be extended over the entire sociopolitical system of the nation, establishing the channels for a veritable polycentric distribution of power, displacing power from the centre towards the periphery, increasing the effective power of decision making and the autonomy of the particular communities and municipalities. The Electoral Assemblies of each municipality and state will elect Electoral Councils which will possess a permanent character and will function in absolute independence from the political parties. They will be able to establish and direct the most diverse mechanisms of Direct Democracy: popular assemblies, referenda, plebiscites, popular initiatives, vetoes, revocation, etc… Thus the concept of *participatory* democracy will be changed into a form in which democracy based on popular sovereignty constitutes itself as the *protagonist* of power. It is precisely at such borders that we must draw the limits of advance of Bolivarian democracy. Then we shall be very near to the territory of *utopia*.[50]

Whether such ideas can be turned into reality or remain utopian ideals cannot be decided within the confines of the political sphere. For the latter is itself in need of the type of radical transformation which foreshadows from the outset the perspective of the "withering away of the state". In Venezuela, where in many parts of the country as much as *90 percent of the population* demonstrates its "rebellion against the absurdity of the vote through its electoral abstention",[51] the traditional political practices and the apologetic legitimatory use to which the "democratic electoral system" is put, falsely claiming for the system the unchallengeable justification of a "mandate conferred by the majority", no condemnation of vacuous parliamentary paternalism can be considered too sharp.

Nor can it be seriously argued that high electoral participation is itself the proof of actually existing democratic popular consensus. After all, in some Western democracies the act of voting is compulsory and may in fact add up in its legitimatory value to no more than the most extreme forms of openly critical or pessimistically resigned abstentionism.

Nevertheless, the measure of validity for subjecting to the necessary radical critique the parliamentary representational system is the strategic undertaking to exercise the "sovereignty of labour" not only in political assemblies, no matter how *direct* they might be with regard to their organisation and mode of political decision making, but in the self-determined productive and distributive life-activity of the social individuals in every single domain and at all levels of the social metabolic process. This is what draws the line of demarcation between the socialist revolution which is socialist in its *intent*—like the October Revolution of 1917—and the *"permanent revolution"* of effective socialist transformation. For without the progressive and ultimately complete transfer of material reproductive and distributive decision making to the associated producers there can be no hope for the members of the postrevolutionary community of transforming themselves into the *subject* of power.

4.4

IN THE second half of the 20th century no one has argued more forcefully in favour of finding legislative guarantees against the abuse of political power and the violation of human rights than Norberto Bobbio. Conscious of the inhumanities committed in the name of socialism under the Soviet-type system, he tried to combine the best features of liberalism with the aspirations of democratic socialism. Firmly rejecting the idea of "direct democracy", he advocated the institution of guarantees and improvements in human rights through the parliamentary legislative system.[52] Significantly, however, the improvement of existing conditions by means of formally guaranteed rights advocated by Bobbio has become progressively more dependent on changing the *material* determinations and imperatives of the capital system. Accordingly, a radical critique of this system as a social metabolic order would seem to be the necessary precondition for assessing the legislative measures compatible with it.

In a 1992 interview Bobbio stressed that in our age the right to liberty and work, coupled with the individual's entitlement to social security provisions, must be complemented by the rights of the present and future generations to live in an unpolluted environment, with the right to self-regulated human procreation and guarantees of privacy against all encroachments on it by the ubiquitous all-controlling state, as well as with legally secured guarantees against the grave dangers increasingly affecting the genetic patrimony.[53] Much as one can agree with all these demands, it is disturbingly clear that even the parliamentary enactment of the advocated rights and guarantees—with the possible exception of the formally proclaimed "right to liberty" which is, however, materially emptied of all content in practice for the overwhelming majority of humankind by the established mode of social metabolic control—would become possible only by successfully confronting the massive material and political vested interests militating against them. Besides, formal enactment would by itself provide no guarantees for their implementation, as countless solemnly proclaimed democratic constitutional principles and just as countless unenforced laws decorating the existing statute books amply testify. For they remain unenforced precisely because they would, or even just might, curtail the power of capital. In a world of chronic unemployment, with constant attacks even on the meagre remnants of the "welfare state" and the social security system, under the pressure to maximally exploit everything, from unrenewable resources to the ethically most questionable advances made in bio- and information-technology in direct subordination to the dictates of profitable capital-accumulation, one could only dream about enforcing the diametrical opposite of such developments by the good offices of an enlightened legislature.

Equally, it would be nothing short of a miracle if a system of reproductive control which is structurally incapable of planning and restraining the harmful impact of its own mode of operation even for the day after tomorrow could codify and respect the rights of *future generations* clearly in conflict with its material imperatives. Naturally, this circumstance does not invalidate the Italian philosopher's point that the left should fight in every way it can to make people conscious of the merits of such demands, as part of its critique of the established social order. But it puts sharply into relief the hopeless limitations of the available legislative institutions for solving the deep-seated material reproductive problems identified by Bobbio himself.

Social democracy in its long history at first followed the path of trying to introduce major changes in the prevailing class relations through parliamentary reform and—after a few decades of failure to advance the objectives of socialist transformation—ended up totally reneging on them. This was by no means accidental or simply due to "personal betrayal" of their erstwhile principles by the socialdemocratic parliamentary representatives. Their enterprise of instituting socialism by parliamentary means was doomed from the outset. For they envisaged the realisation of the *impossible*. They promised to gradually transform into something radically different—that is, into a socialist order—a system of social reproductive control over which they *did not and could not have any meaningful control* in and through parliament.

As we have seen above, capital—by its very nature and innermost determinations—is *uncontrollable*. Therefore, to invest the energies of a social movement into trying to *reform* a substantively *uncontrollable* system, is a much more futile venture than the labour of Sisyphus, since the viability of even the most limited reform is inconceivable without the ability to exercise control over those aspects or dimensions of a social complex which one is attempting to reform. And that is what made the social democratic parliamentary enterprise self-contradictory and doomed from the outset. For the social democratic parties continued to delude themselves and their electors, for decades, that they would be able to institute 'in due course', through parliamentary legislation, a *structural reform of the uncontrollable capital system*.

The blind alley of social democracy was by no means the original path of the socialist movement. Following the road of parliamentary reform and accommodation became the dominant orientation in the political parties of the working class only with the emergence and consolidation of the Second International. Naturally, the blind apologists for the abandonment of all socialist objectives by the present-day leadership of social democratic and labour parties try to retrospectively rewrite history, grotesquely suggesting that:

> The original—and, for its day, audacious—*aim of socialism* was *democratic capitalism*. It was not until the 1840s, when *Marx and Engels hijacked the term*, that "socialism" became a project whose ambition was to destroy capitalism. Clause 4 [of the British Labour party's seventy year old constitution] remains a fundamentally Marxist text, for all its slippery language and the wishes of its authors to distance Labour from the worst excesses of Lenin's dictatorship of the proletariat. Hence the importance of [present leader] Blair's announcement. He is challenging his party, at last, to *bury Marxist socialism*.[54]

The historical facts, wilfully brushed aside by all apologists, speak otherwise. For the radical negation of the capitalist order goes back a long way before Marx and Engels had set their eyes on England. The persecuted secret societies engaged in working-class-oriented negation of the established order's incorrigible—and thus unreformable/"undemocratisable"— structural iniquities go back at least as far as the French Revolution and its turbulent aftermath. As a matter of fact Marx's first acquaintance with the uncompromising demands of radical anti-capitalist socialism took place precisely in such secret working class societies during his stay in France as a young man, well before he started to write his seminal *Economic and Philosophical Manuscript of 1844.* Anybody who can seriously commit to paper the proposition that a world-historical revolutionary movement can be invented by two exiled young German intellectuals who "hijack the term socialism" is as completely out of contact with reality and all sense as someone who can pontificate, just because he fancies it, that by replacing the long held commitment to public ownership in Clause 4 of the Labour party's constitution with the unprincipled verbal concoction of "New Labour", Tony Blair can actually "bury Marxist socialism"—"if he finds the right words", as the wishful projection puts it.

The derailment of the working class movement occurred in the last third of the 19th century, and its negative consequences became pronounced with the parliamentary success—and accommodation—of the social democratic and labour parties. The success itself could only be considered a Pyrrhic victory in its long-term impact on the cause of labour's emancipation. For the price which had to be paid for it was the fateful structural weakening of labour's fighting potential, caused by the acceptance of the parliamentary constraints as the only legitimate framework of contesting the rule of capital. In practical terms this had meant catastrophically dividing the movement into the so-called *"political arm"* and the *"industrial arm"* of labour, with the illusion that the "political arm" would serve or represent, by legislatively codifying, the interests of the class of labour organised in the capitalist industrial enterprises by the particular trade unions of the "industrial arm". As time went by, however, everything turned out to be exactly the other way round. The "political arm", instead of asserting its political mandate in close collaboration with the "industrial arm", used the rules of the parliamentary game in order to subordinate the trade unions to itself and to capital's ultimate political determinations enforced through parliament. Thus, instead of politically strengthening the fighting force of the "industrial arm" in its confrontations with capitalist enterprises, thereby enhancing the emancipatory potential of labour, the "political arm" confined the trade unions—in the name of its own political exclusiveness—to *"strictly economic labour disputes"*. In this way what was supposed to be the "political arm of labour" ended up with playing a crucial part in actively imposing on labour—by the force of "representational parliamentary legislation"—capital's vital interest: to ban *"politically motivated industrial action"* as categorically inadmissible "in a democratic society".

Both reformism and its necessarily precarious achievements were corollaries of this split articulation of the labour movement as "political arm" and "industrial arm". Operating in that split mode—within the comprehensive political command structure of capital as the rational framework of legitimacy and democratic authority—had brought with it the necessary acceptance and internalisation of the *objective material constraints of capital*. At the same time reformist labour retained for a while the contradictory idea that socialist objectives were fully compatible with capital's material constraints. In this spirit it was postulated—by Harold Wilson and other labour leaders—that by "conquering the commanding heights of the economy" it will be possible to realise socialism "one day". In reality "conquering the commanding heights" amounted to nothing more than the nationalisation of bankrupt sectors of capitalist industry, generously compensating their former owners for their worthless assets: a process which could be in any case very easily reversed through parliamentary acts of "privatisation" once their profitability to capital has been secured through generous state investment, financed from tax revenue squeezed out of the common people. Ironically, this road, with its self-contradictory twists and turns, has led from the reformist entrapment of the labour movement to the complete disintegration of social democratic reformism itself, whereby not only the once professed socialist "ultimate aims" had to be openly renounced but even references to the term "socialism" had to be avoided like plague.

Another irony which underlines the perverse logic of parliamentary accommodation within the anti-labour confines of capital's comprehensive political command structure is the fate of the "revolutionary" parties of the Third International. It puts sharply into relief that fundamental *structural* determinations were at work in the clamorous defeats suffered by the institutionalised left in the course of the 20th century. Indeed, to make matters worse, the defeats were suffered despite the deepening crises of the ruling socioeconomic and political order. In this sense, the "Italian road to socialism" and the subsequent "great historic compromise" of the Italian Communist party within the same constraints of parliamentary representation and accommodation, with an identical split between the "political arm" and the "industrial arm" of Italian labour as seen in countries with social democratic and labour parties, proved to be as disastrous for the socialist movement as the disintegration of social democratic varieties of reformism.

Thus, in the light of the bitter historical experience to which labour has been subjected by the failure of the parliamentary parties of both the Second and the Third International, it is not too difficult to see that there can be no hope for an effective rearticulation of socialist radicalism without overcoming the contradictions which necessarily arise from the self-defeating division between the "political arm" and the "industrial arm" of labour. For, paradoxically, the reformist separation and compartmentalisation of labour's "two arms" can only amount to the paralysing *"headlessness"* of the movement: ie to the more or less conscious internalisation of capital's logic both in terms of its material constraints and its legislatively safeguarded "democratic" political regulatory principles. For conformity to the rules of the system aprioristically determines in capital's favour what may and what may not be "rationally disputed and contested" not only in the political domain, but even more so as regards the feasibility of questioning and challenging the established framework of social metabolic reproduction. Thus, as a result of the compartmentalised split in tune with those rules, the "political arm" loses the material power through which the labour movement could effectively counter capital's logic and self-assertive power, and struggle not just for minimal—by the existing structural framework containable and, if need be, reversible—concessions, but for the institution of an alternative social reproductive order. At the same time, while the "political arm" is rendered impotent by depriving itself of the combative material power of productive labour—which is vitally important for capital's continued reproduction—the "industrial arm" is compelled to abandon even the *thought* of legitimately concerning itself not only with major structural change but with any political objective whatsoever. It is forced to settle, instead, for marginal improvements; and even its pursuit of such marginal and partial improvements must be strictly subordinated to the *conjunctural* shifts and limitations of the *particular* units of capital with which the local units of the "industrial arm" are by the law allowed to enter into "economic dispute".

4.5

THE INSURMOUNTABLE problem here is—and remains without a fundamental reorientation of the strategic target of socialist transformation—the nature of power under the rule of capital. Reformist politicians, whether of the social democratic kind or those who fantasised about the "Italian road to socialism" within the crippling confines of actually existing capitalism, never faced up to this problem. Indeed they could not face up to it because doing so would have exposed the unrealisable character of their self-contradictory strategies. For just as they were trying to *reform the uncontrollable*, they also assumed as the leverage through which they would bring about the promised transformation of the established social order a *power that did not and could not exist*. Their postulated leverage could not exist for the simple reason that *the power of total social capital as the controller of social metabolic reproduction is indivisible*, notwithstanding the mystifications perpetuated by bourgeois ideology about "the division of powers" in the political sphere.

Understandably, therefore, the strategies built on the two pillars of (1) *reforming the uncontrollable*, and (2) *"conquering the commanding heights"* of the established system through the leverage of a *non-existent power*, had to end with the self-imposed defeat of the historical left. As we have seen above this had to apply, *mutatis mutandis*, also to the postrevolutionary societies of Soviet type "actually existing socialism". For although the postrevolutionary "personifications of capital" in Soviet type societies did not operate in and through a parliamentary setting, they failed to confront the *uncontrollability of capital* where it massively asserted itself: ie as the regulator of social metabolic reproduction. Thus, given their failure to identify the real target of strategic intervention and restructuring, at the social metabolic level, they tried to exercise power in an extremely voluntaristic way, as an attempt to remedy their actual *powerlessness* with regard to the objective material imperatives and the blindly followed—but increasingly defectively fulfilled—expansionary requirements of the postcapitalist capital system.

The fact that capital as a mode of social metabolic reproduction is uncontrollable—the veritable *causa sui* compatible with "improvements and correctives" only at the level of *effects and consequences*, but not at that of the system's causal foundations, as we have seen already in various contexts—means not only that capital is *unreformable* but also that it *cannot share power* even in the short run with forces aiming to transcend it in the no matter how long a run, as their "ultimate aim". This is why social democratic strategies of "gradual reform" had to come to absolutely nothing in terms of socialist transformatory potential. For as long as capital remains the effective regulator of the social metabolism, the idea of "equal contest" between capital and labour—an idea perpetuated and enhanced by the rituals of parliamentary confrontation of "labour's representatives" with their legislative adversaries: a confrontation of "no contest" whose self-contradictorily accepted premise is the permanence of capital's material ground—is bound to remain a mystification. The limited political disputes in parliament, in the strictly regulated and by the instruments and institutions of "legitimate violence" underpinned framework of capital's comprehensive political command structure, cannot be a *contest with capital* but only *among* its more or less diverse constituents. Those parliamentary constituents which, whether they profess their allegiance to various business interests or to sections of reformist labour, willingly accept their submission to the necessary constraints of defining their legislative objectives in accordance with the self-serving rules of total social capital's "constitutional state". At the same time the representatives of labour who try to maintain a radical critical stance are either kept out of parliament or become totally marginalised in it. In contrast to the parliamentary system the "personifications of capital" in postcapitalist societies operated under a very different but equally harmful mystification. They vainly tried to treat capital either as a *material entity*—the neutral depository of "socialist accumulation"—or as an equally *neutral mechanism: the "social market"*, ignoring that capital is in reality always a *social relation*. Thus the *fetishism of capital* dominated postcapitalist societies as much as it ruled them under capitalism, even if the new rule of capital had to assume a different form.

The relationship between capital and labour cannot be considered *symmetrical*, with the possibility of *balancing the contested power* between the two, let alone of changing it *in labour's favour*. The concept of "balance of power" as the regulator of internal sociopolitical power belongs to the world of capital only, affecting with "legitimate concern" the changing interrelations of the smaller and larger constituents of total social capital as articulated at any particular point in history. The ever-growing "legislative jungle" mentioned in Section 4.3 is the necessary concomitant of this type of structural articulation of social capital as a whole. From this type of articulation—subject to the practical qualifications arising from the monopolistic trend of the system—necessarily follows also the balance-oriented contest *among* particular constituents of capital in the legislative arena. And that includes also the limited possibilities of legislative action accorded to sections of reformist labour on the margins of the constantly renewed and just as constantly overthrown internal balancing contest of capital's changing units. (A good example of this type of balance-oriented marginal improvement is Sir Winston Churchill's "enlightened" legislation in 1906 over *minimum wage* levels "in favour of labour", as well as the recent controversies in the European Union concerning the demand for equal remuneration to be given to groups of labour moving from one member country to another. Naturally, the complete overthrow of the good old "minimum wage legislation" by the "Radical Right" under Margaret Thatcher and her successors, overthrown despite its impeccable Churchillian legislative ancestry, demonstrates the extreme precariousness of such "labour conquests" under significantly altered historical circumstances, just as the present controversy hides the underlying self-protective capital interests and the necessary fragility of labour's measures associated with them.)

While the interests of capital's particular constituents can be successfully—even if strictly temporarily—balanced, there can be no question of balancing the interests and the corresponding power of capital and labour with one another. Labour is either the *structural antagonist and systemic alternative to capital*—in which case "sharing power" with capital is an absurd self-contradiction—or remains the structurally subordinate part (the constantly endangered "cost of production") of capital's expanded self-reproduction process, and as such totally *devoid of power*. The effective power of labour in the existing socioeconomic order is *partial* and *negative,* like the *strike weapon.* Thus it cannot be sustained in its negativity indefinitely, since the necessary practical premise of its operation—even if we are thinking of the quite extraordinary one year long British miners' strike—is the continued functioning of the social metabolic order whose working parts must be able to take over also the burden of temporarily withdrawn labour. The idea of a political general strike is a radically different proposition. If it is to be successful it must have for its objective a fundamental change in the social reproductive order itself, otherwise its impact is bound to be subsequently nullified, as with general strikes in the past. Thus the paradox of power facing the socialist movement is that the exercise of labour's actually existing but *negative* power is unsustainable in the long run even in its *partiality,* and only its *potentially* positive power is truly sustainable, as by its very nature it cannot be confined to the pursuit of *partial* objectives. For the condition of its actualisation is that the positive power of labour as the systemic alternative to capital's mode of control should envisage itself as the radical structuring principle of the social metabolic order as a whole. Thus, whichever way we look at it—whether in its partially contesting negativity or as the positive potentiality of comprehensive socialist transformation—it becomes clear that under no circumstances can one think of the power of labour as shared with capital (or the other way round), notwithstanding the well known illusions and the ensuing necessary defeats of parliamentary reformism.

From the non-symmetrical relationship between capital and labour also follows that—in complete contrast to the practices of representation affecting the internal relations of the plurality of capitals—*labour cannot be represented.* In a sense it is also true that *capital cannot be represented.* But it is true with a radical difference compared to the position of labour. The idea of capital itself being represented in the parliamentary domain can only project the mirage of *shared and balanced power* between *capital and labour,* as we find it in the countless fairy tales of bourgeois and reformist ideology. However, the postulate of "equality" and "fairness", on the ground that neither labour nor capital as such are directly represented in the legislative domain, which is supposed to be regulated by a somewhat mysterious "process of the law itself", in tune with Max Weber's idea that the "jurists" were the autonomous creators of the "Occidental state", is also nothing but a self-serving camouflage of the existing power relations. For the big difference is that capital as a whole is not represented because it *needs no representation since it is already fully in control of the social metabolic process*, including the effective—extra-parliamentary—control of its own comprehensive political command structure, the state. Labour, on the other hand, cannot be represented *in principle*, because its possible forms of "representation"—even if they could be organised in the political sphere on the basis of "fairness" and "justice", which they cannot conceivably be in view of the existing material and ideological power relations—would of necessity remain utterly sterile. For they could not alter the extra-parliamentary structural determinations of capital's profoundly entrenched mode of social metabolic reproduction.

Naturally this does not mean that the historically evolved system of parliamentary representation is irrelevant to the assertion of capital's rule over society. Nor can one indeed see its value to capital only because of its undoubted power of ideological mystification. Far from it. For parliamentary representation is able to fulfil some vitally important functions in the existing social metabolic order. In part the essential regulatory role of parliament consists in legitimating (and thereby also "internalising") the imposition of the strictest rules of "constitutional legality" on potentially recalcitrant labour. But the role of parliament is by no means limited to that. Indeed, in the historical development of parliament making labour submit to self-legitimating "constitutional legality" came second to its original and primary function. That crucial function consisted and consists in enabling the *plurality of capitals* to find the necessary (even if always temporary) *modus vivendi* and *balance of power among themselves* at any given temporal slice of the system's unfolding dynamics. This is how capital as total social capital can assert its rule in the political sphere under the conditions of "parliamentary democracy".

As we have seen above, the capital system is made up from incorrigibly *centrifugal* constituents, on the basis of an equally incorrigible *adversarial* structural relationship common to all of its parts, from the smallest reproductive "microcosms" to the

biggest transnational corporations. It is capital as a social totality which brings under control (and *must* do so in a suitable
way) the centrifugal force. It can do this through those universally prevailing rules and structural determinations which
objectively define capital itself as a mode of social metabolic
control. The determinations in question are *internal* not only to
the system as a whole but also to all of its parts. In other words,
they must be *shared* by all of capital's manifold particular constituents, notwithstanding their conflicting interests vis-à-vis
one another. Without sharing them—which simultaneously
also means sharing the vital *common interest* to be parts of the
controlling system of social metabolic reproduction, from
which the self-interested class consciousness of the "personifications of capital" arises—they could not operate among
themselves as a plurality of capitals asserting their particular
interests within the overall structural constraints and self-pre-
serving dynamism of their system in any given historical
situation. This is how capital as such, articulated as the actually
existing mode of social metabolic reproduction, can bring
under control the untranscendable centrifugal force of its constituent parts. Not by simply *overruling* that force—whereby the
capital system would cease to be a viable system *sui generis*—
but by *complementing* it through the imperative of overall
systemic reproduction, thereby restraining only the *disintegrative* impact of the insurmountable *conflictual* interactions.

This is how the state of the capital system acquires its great
importance not simply as the overall regulatory framework of
contingent *political* relations but as an essential material constituent of the system in its entirety, without which capital could
not assert itself as the controlling power of the established mode
of social metabolic reproduction. Accordingly, under the circumstances of "constitutional democracy" the parliamentary
system is an essential part of bringing the centrifugal force of
the plurality of capitals under suitable control. In this process
the interests of the multiplicity of capitals can be adequately represented. For the representation of even the most diverse capital
interests in parliament, under the comprehensive political command structure of capital, is fully in tune with the overall
determinations of social metabolic control. Apart from the
structural antagonism between capital and labour which affects,

of course, also capital's particular constituents, the conflicts of the plurality of capitals are played out—subject to the restraining overall determinations mentioned above—among themselves. They can *never* be directed against the capital *system* without which the plurality of conflicting capitals cannot be even imagined, let alone exist. Thus the regulatory force of parliamentary representation, as far as the plurality of capitals is concerned, is fully adequate both as genuine *representation* and as the *preservation* (or "eternalisation") of a power—the power of social metabolic control—*already in existence*. But precisely for that reason, labour cannot be represented in principle. For the vital interest of labour is the *radical transformation* of the established social reproductive order, and not its *preservation*: the only thing compatible with parliamentary representation as such under the comprehensive political command structure of capital. This is how the non-symmetrical relation between capital and labour nullifies the emancipatory interests of labour in the political sphere under all historically known forms of the parliamentary system.

There is another way in which parliamentary politics serves the interests of capital as a metabolic system as well as the interests of its manifold constituents. For according to the changing dynamics of development of total social capital, parliament can provide the framework of quite far-reaching shifts in the system's strategic operation vis-à-vis labour, such as the move from the postwar decades of "Butskellism" (or paternalistic "one-nation Toryism") to the savagery of Thatcherite "Radical Right" strategies. Highly revealing in this respect is the sharp contrast between two parliamentary solutions to capital's unfolding structural crisis as perceived and commended by different sections of British capital in 1979. For the same year which had initiated the already fifteen year long domination of British parliament by Margaret Thatcher's government had also witnessed the eclipse of the earlier political line of the Conservative party, as encapsulated in a nostalgic interview broadcast on BBC Television by former Prime Minister Harold Macmillan in February 1979. This is how "Super-Mac"—who later sarcastically denounced the Thatcher government on account of its corrupt privatisation policies as a short-sighted and vulgar practice of "selling off the family silver"—summed up his proposed solution to the no longer deniable crisis, trying to remain in tune with the spirit of Keynesian welfare state oriented "consensus politics" followed by the dominant sections of British capital after the Second World War for two and a half decades:

> So perhaps the way would be somehow to get everybody together and say, *"Boys, it's all in our hands*; let's get down and do it, add to the total production of *marketable wealth"*. That's what we want… On the home side, I am sure people would welcome a real lead—*"Boys and girls, let's get together* and make this marvellous world we could make for ourselves"… I am quite certain that there are forces now which, if we could only get them to *unite, whether in government or unity of the great organisations of employers and trade unions*, or the churches—all the people who influence opinion—who would say "It's enough; we must make a *new start"*. It's a *moral issue*; we must have the determination and we must rebuild our courage.[55]

A few months after this interview, the Conservative party under Margaret Thatcher's leadership was elected to government. Within a short period of time *all* of the "one-nation" Tory members of parliament were condemned as 'wets' and consigned to the political wilderness as brutally as the left-wing members of the Labour party were later, under the leadership of former left-wingers Michael Foot and Neil Kinnock. Far from addressing themselves to the "boys and girls" in order to urge them to unite with government and with the "great organisations of employers and trade unions", for the sake of the "moral issue" of making together "a new start" in the improved "production of marketable wealth", the *change of guard* in the Conservative party (and not only in that party) had put as the principal item on the political agenda the "constitutional" oppression of the defensive organs of the working class. The "boys and girls" in parliament—Macmillan's former colleagues—were busy introducing punitive anti-labour laws, coupled with appropriate industrial and financial measures conceived and instituted in the same spirit in favour of capital. And the shift from the political dominance of some sections of capital to more aggressive ones was by no means a British development only. On the contrary, the unfolding structural crisis of the capital system had brought with it very similar political, industrial and financial measures, as well as their ideological rationalisations, everywhere in the "advanced capitalist" countries.

Hard as it may be to believe our eyes when we read the passage quoted below, we have to pay attention to it as a typical example coming from the "Radical Right" in the US. It encapsulates the "objective economic theory" of a leading American financial expert/speculator and influential lobbyist, James Dale Davidson.[56] He argues the "scientific" merits of the anti-labour line in this way:

> As an investor, you should be always wary of commonly held presumptions about economic relationships. This is especially true for a topic like [surprise, surprise!] wages, when special pleading and political considerations stand in the way of the truth. The truth is that whatever their intentions, employers in market societies have a devil of a time "exploiting" the workers. Indeed, this is almost impossible where workers are free to develop their talents and move from one opportunity to another. [ie in the never-nowhere-land of "people's capitalist" utopia.] Surprisingly [this time a real surprise], it is far more common for workers to exploit capitalists. In general, this is the function that labour unions perform. They raise wage rates above the market-clearing level. The result is that investors receive a smaller portion of the revenue of the firm than they would otherwise...the existence of democratic institutions during periods when technology increases scale economies more or less guarantees that the workers will exploit the capitalists.[57]

Characteristically, the ruthless intervention of "democratic parliaments" in undermining even the limited defensive power of trade unions is not even mentioned in the description of the unfolding changes instituted in capital's favour, from the large-scale casualisation of the labour force to the concomitant criminalisation of those who fight against it. Everything is ascribed with customary scientific objectivity to strictly *techno-logical* factors. As if the political forces which the author as lobbyist is eager to influence with all means at his disposal did not exist at all. Thus the anti-union laws of the recent past are supposed to be totally irrelevant to understanding these developments. We are told that rationally unobjectionable technology alone "explains why *unions are now faltering* in Western societies, as technology is reducing scale economies. It explains why *income differentials are widening* once more, as essentially unskilled workers are obliged to find employment at market-clearing wages".[58] That is, in reality, "obliged to find employment" *if they can*, not at "market-clearing wages" but often at well below subsistence-level wages, given the devastating impact of *chronic unemployment* in the idealised "properly scaled economies" of the contemporary capital system. Evidently, all this has nothing to do either with the savagery of anti-union laws or with the dehumanising brutality of "structural unemployment". Indeed, unemployment itself must be the most cunning device ever devised by labour to "exploit the capitalists and investors", poor helpless dears, by obliging them to "receive a smaller portion of the revenue than they would otherwise"; otherwise, being, if the unemployed allowed them to operate the economy under the more generously revenue-producing conditions of full employment.

However, coming back to reality from the carefully crafted fantasy-world of cynical capital-apologetics, there are two further aggravating conditions to be considered here. The first is that labour accommodating itself to the paralysing constraints of the parliamentary framework at the time of capital's deepening structural crisis cannot help being gravely affected by the negative impact of the shifts within total social capital's power structure and by the narrowing margin of action which they can provide to labour even for the most limited defensive gains. Reformist labour's present-day submission to forces diametrically opposed to the interests of the working classes demonstrates that the historical phase of defensive strategies has run its course. The social democratisation of the Western Communist parties, coupled with the transformation of the traditional social democratic and labour parties into the mildest possible advocates of Lib-Labouring—and even in its own terms of reference ineffective—puny socioeconomic and political reform, offer painfully obvious illustrations of the defeat suffered by the historical left through these shifts and changes within the constraints of parliamentary accommodation. The fact that some prominent right-wing politicians of the British Labour party now find themselves marginalised for their "unacceptably outspoken left-wing views", said to damage the prospects of "New Labour" in government—indeed unacceptable to the extent that they themselves feel obliged to announce their retirement from active politics at the next general election, avoiding thereby the humiliation of "deselection"—is an ironical twist in this unhappy but most eloquent cautionary tale. It underlines in its own way, through the party leadership's adopted "preparation for government" which cannot tolerate even the unfulfilled promises of the old Clause 4, that whenever reformist Labour may be in government, capital always remains in charge.

The second aggravating condition is even more serious, in that it calls into question the very survival of humanity. For despite the worsening socioeconomic conditions and the elimination of the margin of even minor adjustments in favour of labour—with the active involvement of authoritarian legislative measures and the complicity of its own party—capital is unable to solve its structural crisis and successfully reconstitute the conditions of expansionary dynamics. On the contrary. In order to remain in control of the social metabolism at all, it is compelled to encroach over territories which it cannot control and utilise for the purposes of sustainable capital-accumulation. Moreover, for the sake of remaining in charge of societal reproduction, at whatever cost to humankind, capital must undermine even its own political institutions which in the past could function as a partial corrective and as some sort of safety valve. In a past, that is, when the road of expansionary displacement of capital's accumulating contradictions was still more or less wide open. Today, by contrast, the options of the capital system are being narrowed down everywhere, including the domain of politics and parliamentary adjustive action. This narrowing down of the options of expansionary recovery brings with it the imperative to directly dominate politics also by a most unholy "consensus politics" between age-old capital and

"New Labour", in fitting complement to the authoritarian tendencies of the "New World Order" by no means only in the British Labour party. The consummation of this unholy consensus—far from being capital's ultimate triumph, as the absurd fantasies about the "end of conflictual history" predicated it—would foreshadow the danger of a major collapse, affecting not only a limited number of capital's centrifugal constituents, and not even just a key strategic sector like international finance, but the global capital system in its entirety. The need for countering the destructive extra-parliamentary force of capital by the appropriate extra-parliamentary action of a radically rearticulated socialist movement acquires its relevance and urgency precisely in view of this danger.

4.6

WHEN THE historical phase of defensive gains is exhausted, labour as the structural antagonist of capital can only advance its cause—even minimally—if it goes on the offensive, envisaging as its strategic target the radical negation and the positive transformation of the mode of social metabolic reproduction also when fighting for the realisation of more limited objectives. For only through the adoption of a viable overall strategy can the partial steps become cumulative, in sharp contrast to all known forms of labour reformism which disappeared without a trace like a few drops of water in the desert sand.

Defensive gains in the past were always closely tied to expansionary phases of the capital system. They were carved out from the margin of concessions which the system could not only afford but also positively turn to its advantage. Even under the most favourable circumstances they could not bring the promised "gradual" realisation of socialism one inch nearer. For by their very nature they could be only *conjunctural concessions*, affordable under conditions favourable to capital itself and only by "reflected glory" helpful also to labour. Once, however, the historical phase of capital's expansionary concessions is left behind, the total capitulation of reformist labour we witnessed in the last few decades accompanies it. This is because under such conditions not only further defensive gains

by labour are out of the question, but even many of the past
concessions must be clawed back, subject only to the potential
destabilising impact on capital's continued self-reproduction if
too much is taken back within a short space of time. This is
what moderates the tendency for the equalisation of the differential rate of exploitation in the capitalistically advanced
countries for as long as the total social capital of the countries
concerned can compensate for it through its neo-colonial domination of areas of the planet which provide for "metropolitan
capital", thanks to a higher rate of practicable exploitation, a
much higher rate of profit. Nevertheless, even such currently
alleviating factors are bound to be temporary and displaced
with the unfolding of capital's structural crisis.

There are some people—who fancy themselves as "realists"—who insist (with slogans like "the party is over") that the
experienced constraints affecting the system must be accepted
as permanent, asking us to accept also the permanence of
labour's structural subordination to capital. They think that
the radical phase of labour militancy is gone forever, adding
that even in the past it was nothing but a big mistake and a
romantic illusion at best; not to mention the "theorists" and
"spin-doctors" of "New Labour" who ascribe the past revolutionary aspirations of the socialist movement to the
"word-highjacking" skills of young Marx and Engels.

The trouble with the ideas of those who postulate the permanent submission of labour to the rule of capital is that they
must also hypostatise the absolute permanence of the capital
system. And that can be done only by totally blinding oneself
even to the most destructive aspects of capital's mode of social
metabolic control, which are visible not only to socialists but
to all those who are willing to make the most elementary envi-
ronmental calculations. The strategic perspective of reformist
labourism was in the past untroubled by such concerns, and
therefore the distinction between "the rule of society over
wealth" as opposed to the alienating "rule of wealth over society" could have no meaning whatsoever for it. However, today
these problems cannot be ignored any longer. Nor is it possible
to equate necessarily self-deflating and disintegrating labour
reformism with labour itself. As should be obvious enough by
now, the history of labour reformism is characterised by its

progressive accommodatory integration into the political command structure of capital, and thus also by its *complete disintegration through its capitulatory integration even as reformism.*

In this way the "realists" who project the unproblematical harmony between capital and social democractic labour simply beg the question. For only accommodatory reformist labour can be imagined in unproblematical harmony with capital, tying itself to the destiny of the latter not only during the system's historical ascendancy but even in its destructive and disintegrative phase of development. This conception also shows a singular inability to see that the class of labour itself cannot avoid being the *structural antagonist of capital,* even if under conditions favouring the reformist perspective—ie when labour's defensive gains can be readily conceded by capital and used for the purposes of its dynamic accumulatory expansion—the demands of social democratic labour can be reconciled with and contained well within the limits of the system. All this is, however, radically altered when the road of dynamic expansion is blocked (for whatever reason), and labour is expected to subject forever its aspirations—even when they directly arise from its elementary needs—to the imperatives of capital's "reason", preached by its own reformist leaders as "necessary realism". Under such altered conditions, if prolonged (as they must be on account of the system's structural crisis), the antagonist of capital is compelled to contemplate the feasibility of a strategic offensive aimed at the radical transformation of the established social metabolic order. It is compelled to do this sooner or later, even if the process of reassessing the strategic orientation of the socialist movement is bound to be a difficult one. For it will have to assume the form of learning from frustrated attempts and disappointed expectations, though hopefully also from a progressively improved approximation to the proper organisational framework and tactical measures through which the adopted strategic targets can be reached.

Another argument which is often used in favour of permanent accommodation is the threat of extreme authoritarian measures that must be faced by a socialist revolutionary movement. This argument is backed up by emphasising both the immense destructive power at capital's disposal and the

undeniable historical fact that no ruling order ever cedes willingly its position of command over society, using if need be
even the most violent form of repression to retain its rule.
The weakness of this argument is twofold, despite the factual
circumstances which would seem to support it.

First, it disregards that the antagonistic confrontation
between capital and labour is not a political/military one in
which one of the antagonists could be slaughtered on the bat-
tlefield or riveted to chains. Inasmuch as there can be chains
in this confrontation, labour is wearing them already, in that
the only type of chains compatible with the system must be
"flexible" enough to enable the class of labour to produce and
be exploited. Nor can one imagine that the authoritarian
might of capital is likely to be used only against a revolutionary socialist movement. The repressive anti-labour measures
of the last two decades—not to mention many instances of
past historical emergency characterised by the use of violence
under the capital system—give a foretaste of worse things to
come in the event of extreme confrontations. But this is not a
matter of either/or, with some sort of apriori guarantee of a
"fair" and benevolent treatment in the event of labour's willing accommodation and submission. The matter hinges on
the gravity of the crisis and on the circumstances under which
the antagonistic confrontations unfold. Uncomfortable as this
truth may sound to socialists, one of the heaviest chains
which labour has to wear today is that it is *tied to capital* for its
continued survival, for as long as it does not succeed in
making a strategic break in the direction of a transition to a
radically different social metabolic order. But that is even
more true of capital, with the qualitative difference that capital cannot make any break towards the establishment of a
different social order. For capital, truly, "there is no alternative"—and there can never be—to its exploitative structural
dependency on labour. If nothing else, this fact sets well
marked limits to capital's ability to permanently subdue
labour by violence, compelling it to use, instead, the earlier
mentioned "flexible chains" against the class of labour. It can
use violence with success selectively, against limited groups of
labour, but not against the socialist movement organised as a
revolutionary *mass movement*. This is why the development of

"communist mass consciousness" (to use Marx's expression), in contrast to the vulnerability of narrow sectarian orientation, is so important.

The second point that must be made in this context is equally important. It concerns the innermost determinations of the capital system as a necessarily expansion-oriented and accumulation-driven social metabolic order. The point is that the exercise of power through the repressive machinery of violence is extremely wasteful in the system's own terms of reference; even if undoubtedly it can serve the purpose of redressing the power relations in capital's favour in a situation of *emergency*. What must weigh heavily in the balance is that it is impossible to secure the required expansion and capital-accumulation on a permanent basis through the perpetuation of economically wasteful emergency, apart from its anything but negligible political dangers. The idea of "Big Brother" successfully ruling over labour as a permanent condition is too fantastic even for a work of Orwellian fiction, let alone for the actuality of capital's mode of social metabolic reproduction. For the latter must perish if it is unable to secure its own reproduction through the appropriation of the fruits of ever more productive labour and the concomitant expanded realisation of value, which in its turn is inconceivable without a dynamic process of "productive consumption". And neither ever-improving labour productivity, with the necessarily increasing socialisation of the labour process as its precondition, nor the required—ever-expanding—scale of "productive consumption" is compatible with the idea of a permanent state of emergency. Moreover, as Chomsky rightly argued many years ago, the surveillance system that must go with a successful enforcement of permanent authoritarian rule involves the absurdity (and, of course, the corresponding cost) of *infinite regress* in monitoring not only the population at large but also the monitoring personnel itself, as well as the monitors of the monitors,[59] etc.

We must add here that the idea of capital's permanent rule through the use of violence must also postulate the total *unity of global capital* against the *national* labour forces which happen to be effectively under the control of capital's particular units in the existing (but by no means unified) global order. This vacuous postulate of capital's global unity and uniformity arbitrarily brushes aside not only the *law of uneven development*. It also ignores the abundant historical evidence which shows that the exercise of force on a mass scale—through war—always needed masses of people to be able to impose violence on their counterparts, motivated as a rule for many centuries by national rivalries. Indeed, the national articulation of the global capital system, far from being a historical accident, had a great deal to do with capital's need to maintain control over the labour force with at least some degree of consensus. Otherwise the inter-capitalist rivalries, all the way to the most comprehensive international conflagrations, would be unmanageably risky from the point of view of total social capital, nullifying the inner logic of the system to fight out to the full the conflict of interests and make the strongest prevail in the Hobbesian *bellum omnium contra omnes*. For in every situation of major inter-capitalist confrontation the capital system itself would be in danger of being overthrown by its labour antagonist, in the absence of a sufficiently high degree of consensus—present as a rule to a very high degree in national conflicts—between capital and labour belonging to the same side. (In fact some radical socialists tried to counter this consensus, unsuccessfully, with the programme inviting the workers at the outbreak of the First World War "to turn their weapons against their national bourgeoisie".)

Thus, to sum up, all of the arguments in favour of capital's permanent rule through the imposition of violence on a mass scale suffer from having to define their conditions of realisation in a self-contradictory way. Accordingly, as mentioned in Section 2.5, to project the rule of capital, in its direct antagonistic confrontation with labour, by way of a completely *unstable*, hence *necessarily transient*, state of *emergency*, as the *permanent* condition of its future *normality*, is a mind-boggling notion. To be sure, no one should doubt that the use of violence may *postpone* for a shorter or longer period of time the success of labour's positive emancipatory efforts; but it cannot *prevent* the exhaustion of capital's productive potentialities. On the contrary, if anything, it can only *accelerate* their exhaustion if violence is used on a mass scale, thereby radically undermining the objective conditions of capital's rule.

THE GREAT difficulty for labour as the antagonist of capital is that while the only viable target of its transformatory struggle must be the social metabolic power of capital—with its not simply personal but objective structural/hierarchical control over the material productive sphere, from which other forms of "personification" may (and as time goes by under misconceived strategies also *must*) arise—this all-important target cannot be reached without gaining control over the political sphere. Moreover, the difficulty is compounded by the temptation to believe that once the political institutions of the inherited capitalist system are neutralised, the power of capital is itself firmly under control: a fateful belief which could only lead to the well known historical defeats of the past.

The capital system is made up from incorrigibly *centrifugal* constituents, complemented as their *cohesive* dimension not only by the unceremoniously overruling power of the "invisible hand" but also by legal and political functions of the modern state. The failure of postcapitalist societies was that they tried to counter the centrifugal structuring determination of the inherited system by *superimposing* on its particular adversarial constituents the *extreme centralised command structure* of an authoritarian political state. This they did in place of addressing the crucial problem of how to *remedy*—through internal restructuring and the institution of *substantive democratic control*—the adversarial character and the concomitant centrifugal mode of functioning of the particular reproductive and distributive units. The removal of the private capitalist personifications of capital therefore could not fulfil its role even as the *first step* on the road of the promised socialist transformation. For the adversarial and centrifugal nature of the inherited system was in fact retained through the superimposition of centralised political control at the expense of labour. Indeed, the social metabolic system was rendered more uncontrollable than ever before as a result of the inability to productively replace the "invisible hand" of the old reproductive order by the voluntaristic authoritarianism of the "visible" new personifications of postcapitalist capital. Inevitably, this brought with it the growing hostility of the mistreated subjects of politically extracted surplus-labour towards the postrevolutionary order. The fact that the labour force was subjected to ruthless political control, and at times even to the most inhuman discipline of mass labour camps, does not mean that the Soviet type personifications of capital were in control of their system. The uncontrollability of the postcapitalist reproductive system manifested itself through its chronic failure to reach its economic targets, making a mockery of its claims regarding the "planned economy". This is what sealed its fate, depriving it of its professed legitimation and making its collapse only a matter of time. That in the final stages of existence of the Soviet type system the postrevolutionary personifications of capital desperately tried to smuggle into their societies the "invisible hand" by the back door, rebaptising it—in order to make it palatable—as *"market socialism"*, could only underline how hopelessly uncontrollable the postcapitalist system had remained even after seven decades of "socialist control", in the total absence of a substantive democratic control of its productive and distributive units.

It stands to reason that the reconstitution and substantive democratisation of the political sphere is a necessary condition for making an inroad into capital's mode of social metabolic control. For the power of capital is not, and cannot be, confined to the direct productive functions. In order to successfully control the latter, capital must be complemented by its own mode of political control. The material command structure of capital cannot assert itself without the system's comprehensive political command structure. Thus, the alternative to capital's mode of social metabolic control must likewise embrace all complementary aspects of the societal reproduction process, from the direct productive and distributive functions to the most comprehensive dimensions of political decision making. Since capital is *actually* in control of all vital aspects of the social metabolism, it can afford to define the sphere of political legitimation as a strictly *formal* matter, thereby apriori excluding the possibility of being legitimately challenged in its *substantive* sphere of operation. Conforming to such determinations, labour as the antagonist of actually existing capital can only condemn itself to permanent impotence. For the institution of a viable alternative social metabolic order is feasible only through the articulation of *substantive democracy*, defined as the self-determined activity of the associated producers in politics no less than in material and cultural production.

It is a unique feature of the capital system that, as a matter of normality, the material reproductive functions are carried on in a separate compartment, under a command structure substantially different from capital's comprehensive political command structure embodied in the modern state. This separation and "diremption", as constituted in the course of capital's historical ascendancy in its orientation for self-expanding exchange-value, is in no way disadvantageous to the system itself. Quite the contrary. For the economic/managerial personifications of capital can exercise their authority over the particular reproductive units, in anticipation of a feed-back from the market, to be translated in due course into corrective action, and the state fulfils its complementary functions partly in the international sphere of the world market (including the safeguard of capital-interests in wars if need be), and partly vis-à-vis the potentially or actually recalcitrant labour force. Thus on both counts the structural antagonist of capital is firmly kept under control by the established compartmentalisation and the radical alienation of the power of decision making—in all spheres—from the producers in a system well suited to the requirements of capital's expanded reproduction and accumulation.

In complete contrast, the alternative—socialist—mode of reproductive control is unimaginable without successfully overcoming the existing diremption and alienation. For the necessary condition of carrying out the direct material reproductive functions of a socialist system is the restitution of the power of decision making—in all spheres of activity and at all levels of co-ordination, from the local productive enterprises to the most comprehensive international interchanges—to the associated producers. Thus the "withering away of the state" refers to nothing mysterious or remote but to a perfectly tangible process which must be initiated right in the present. It means the progressive reacquisition of the alienated powers of political decision making by the individuals in their transition towards a genuine socialist society. Without the reacquisition of these powers neither the new mode of political control of society as a whole by its individuals is conceivable, nor indeed the non-adversarial and thereby cohesive/plannable everyday operation of the particular productive and distributive units by their self-managing associated producers.

The reconstitution of the unity of the material reproductive and the political sphere is the essential defining characteristic of the socialist mode of social metabolic control. Creating the necessary mediations towards it cannot be left to some far-away future time, like the apologetically theorised "highest stage of communism". For if the mediatory steps are not pursued right from the outset, as an organic part of the transformatory strategy, they will be never taken. Keeping the political dimension under a separate authority, divorced from the material reproductive functions of the labour force means retaining the structural dependency and subordination of labour, making thereby also impossible to take the subsequent steps in the direction of a sustainable socialist transformation of the established social order. It was in this sense both revealing and fateful that the Soviet system *reinforced* the separate state functions against the labour force under its control, superimposing the *dictates* of its political apparatus on the direct productive processes under the pretext of "planning", instead of helping to activate the autonomous power of decision making of the producers. Even the time scale of eternity could not turn a social metabolic order trapped by such hopelessly alienating structural determinations into a self-managed socialist system.

4.7

UNDER THE circumstances of actually existing "advanced capitalism" the worsening condition of the labour force cannot be countered—let alone the painful structural dependency of labour challenged—without a fundamental rearticulation of the socialist movement from its defensive posture to one capable of offensive action. For not only the traditional parliamentary mode of political control but also the reformist accommodation of labour within it have run their historical course.

What is important to bear in mind here is that the renewal of the parliamentary form of political legislation itself is unavoidable if the labour movement is to achieve anything at all under the present circumstances. Such a renewal can only come about through the development of an *extra-parliamentary* movement

as the *vital conditioning force* of parliament itself and of the legislative framework of transitional society in general. As things
stand today, labour as the antagonist of capital is forced to
defend its interests not with one but with both hands tied
behind its back. One tied by forces openly hostile to labour and
the other by its own reformist party and trade union leadership.
The latter fulfil their special functions as personifications of capital within the labour movement itself in the service of total
accommodation, and indeed capitulation, to the "realistic"
material imperatives of the system. What is left, then, under the
present crippling articulation of the mass labour movement as
the only weapon to carry on the fight with—head-butting
against steel spikes—is not what one might consider to be suitable even as a strictly defensive weapon; despite the fact that the
spokespersons of "New Labour" enlist the services of "the great
and the good" of capitalist society in their "Justice
Commissions" in order to proclaim that the ongoing contest
fully conforms to the requirements of "fairness" and "justice".
Under these conditions the alternative facing the labour movement is either to resign itself to the acceptance of such
constraints, or to take the necessary steps to untie its own
hands, no matter how hard that course of action might be. For
nowadays the former reformist leaders of labour openly admit,
as Tony Blair did it in a speech delivered in Derby appropriately
on April Fool's day, that "The Labour party is *the party of modern
business* and industry in Britain".[60] This represents the final phase
of the total betrayal of everything belonging to the old social
democratic tradition that could be betrayed. As we can read in
The Times of London:

> Labour, in its famous "prawn cocktail" strategy of City
> lunches [under former leader John Smith], has
> approached business before. But the new commission
> [on "Public Policy and British Business", set up by
> Labour on the model of its "Justice Commission"], espe-
> cially in its arm's-length relationship with the party, is
> different. "The idea of the 'prawn cocktail' offensive was
> to show that we didn't mean harm", says one Blair col-
> league. "This goes beyond that: we want to show that *we
> can do business with business*".[61]

The only question is, how long will the class of labour allow itself to be treated as April's Fool, and how long can the strategy of capitulating to big business be pursued beyond the coming Pyrrhic electoral victory. After all, we know not only that Margaret Thatcher could "do business with Gorbachev", and *vice versa*, in the same spirit of "there is no alternative" which is now being championed by "New Labour" as "the party of modern business". We also know what happened to both Gorbachev and Baroness Thatcher in the end, as well as to their once glorified strategies.

The contest between capital and labour within the framework of the parliamentary system was never "fair and equal", nor could it ever be. For capital as such is not a *parliamentary force*, despite the fact that its interests can be properly represented in parliament, as mentioned before. What necessarily prejudges against labour the political confrontation with capital confined to parliament is the incorrigible circumstance that total social capital cannot help being the *extra-parliamentary force par excellence*. This remains so even when the representatives of the plurality of capitals assert the interests of their system as a whole against labour, and also sort out the legal/political regulatory aspects of their particular differences of interest among themselves, with the help of the "parliamentary rules of the game".

Naturally, when it comes to imposing the dictates of capital on the parliamentary governments of labour, no nonsense can be tolerated from Labour prime ministers. Nearly ten years ago Sir Campbell Adamson—a former Director General of the Confederation of British Industry—made a telling confession in a television interview. He revealed that he had actually threatened Harold Wilson (at the time Labour prime minister of the British Government) with a *general investment strike* if Wilson failed to respond positively to the ultimatum of his Confederation. Adamson candidly admitted that the threatened action would have been *unconstitutional* (in his own words), adding that "fortunately" in the end there was no need to proceed with the planned investment strike because "the prime minister agreed to our demands".

Thus *constitutionality* itself is a plaything for the representatives of capital, to be ruthlessly and cynically used as a self-legitimating device against labour. The personifications of capital, when they abuse "democratic constitutionality", are, of course, not sent to the Tower of London, as they undoubtedly would have been for an equivalent outrage against their king in the late Middle Ages. On the contrary, they are knighted or elevated to the House of Lords, even by Labour Governments. As to the people who might think that this is the "peculiarity of the English", they should remember what happened to the President—the *ex officio* guardian of the American Constitution—in the much talked about "Irangate Contra Affair". The US Congressional Committee investigating that affair had concluded that the Reagan Administration was guilty of *"subverting the Law and undermining the Constitution"*. But, of course, this judgement—despite its grave implications for the professed "rule of law" (never noticed by the Hayeks of this world), did not affect in the slightest the guilty "Teflon President"; nor did it result in the introduction of the required constitutional safeguards in order to prevent similar violations of the US Constitution in the future.

As far as the political representatives of labour are concerned, the issue is not simply that of personal failure or yielding to the temptations and rewards of their privileged position when they are in office. It is much more serious than that. The trouble is that when as heads or Ministers of governments they are supposed to be able to politically control the system they do nothing of the kind. For they operate within the political domain *apriori* prejudged in capital's favour by the existing power structures of its mode of social metabolic reproduction. Without radically challenging and materially dislodging capital's deeply entrenched structures and mode of social metabolic control, *capitulation* to the power of capital is only a question of time; as a rule almost managing to outpace the speed of light. Whether we think of Ramsay MacDonald and Bettino Craxi, or Felipe Gonzáles and François Mitterrand—and even long imprisoned Nelson Mandela, the new-found champion of the South African arms industry[62]—the story is always depressingly the same. Often even the wishful anticipation of the "realistic and responsible role" which is supposed to be appropriate to an expected future high ministerial position is enough to produce the most astonishing somersaults. Thus Aneurin Bevan, once the idol of the Labour left and the most fiery opponent of the nuclear arms race in Britain, did not hesitate to denude himself of his socialist principles and shout down his former left-wing comrades at the party's annual policy-making conference, saying that as the designated foreign secretary of a future Labour Government he could not be expected "to walk into the international negotiating chamber naked, and sit around the conference table like that while defending the interests of the country", ie the privileged position of British imperialism as a member of the exclusive "nuclear club".

The working class was an "afterthought" to the bourgeois parliamentary system, and was always treated by it in that way after entering its corridors. For it could never even remotely match capital's power as the effective material foundation of the parliamentary political system. Even if the formal rules and the material costs of entering parliament could be made equitable—which, of course, they cannot be, in view of the monstrous inequality of wealth between the classes, as well as the educational and ideological advantages enjoyed by the ruling class as the material and cultural controller of the "ruling ideology"—even that would not significantly alter the situation. For the fundamental question concerns the *structural* relationship between the parliamentary political framework and the existing mode of social metabolic reproduction totally dominated by capital.

The diremption of economics and politics which eminently suited the historical development of the capital system presented, by contrast, an enormous challenge to the labour movement, which it could not meet. The failure of the historical left was inextricably tied to this circumstance. For the defensive articulation of the socialist movement both directly *reflected* and *accommodated itself* to this diremption. The fact that the fateful acceptance of such structural determinations was not a gladly, voluntarily undertaken act but a *forced accommodation* does not alter the fact of labour's entrapment by the available, hopelessly narrow, margins of self-emancipatory action within the given framework. It was a forced accommodation in the sense that it was imposed upon labour as the *necessary precondition* for being allowed to enter the parliamentary domain of "political emancipation" and corresponding limited reformist material improvements, once that road was embarked upon by the originally extra-parliamentary radical oppositional forces. The space for this type of reformist articulation of the mass labour movement was opened up in the "European little corner of the world", with its imperialistically dominated global "hinterland", by the dynamic expansionary—and thus affordably "permissive"—phase of capital's development in the second half of the 19th century, and it took almost a century to run its historical course.

The hopelessly paralysing separation of the "political arm" and the "industrial arm" of labour mentioned earlier was an appropriate complement to and support of this type of development, offering in a most discriminatory way some limited material advantages to the working classes of a handful of privileged countries at the expense of the super-exploited masses in the rest of the world. The projection that a *radical structural change*—socialism achieved by gradual reform—would one day arise from the unquestionable *acceptance of the incorrigible structural constraints of the system* was a delusion right from the beginning, even if at first some reformist politicians and trade union leaders genuinely believed in it. It was, of course, a contingent historical fact that the socialist movement, after very different beginnings, accepted the separation of its "political arm" from its industrial body, in order to be able to operate within the parliamentary framework created by the personifications of capital for defending and managing the interests of the capital system. However, the triumph of the reformist strategy in the socialist movement was by no means accidental or the consequence of contingent personal aberrations and bureaucratic betrayals. It was the inevitable concomitant of fitting the movement into the preestablished parliamentary political framework and accommodating it to the peculiar structural diremption between politics and economics characteristic of the capital system.

The success of the socialist offensive is inconceivable without radically challenging these structural determinations of the established order and without reconstituting the labour movement in its integrality; not only with its "arms" but also with the full consciousness of its transformatory objective as the necessary and feasible strategic alternative to the capital system.

4.8

THE INSOLUBLE problem within the existing framework of political institutions is the fundamental inequality between capital and labour in the material power relations of society as a whole, asserting itself for as long as the established mode of metabolic reproduction is not radically altered. It is important to quote in this respect a passage from Marx's *Economic Manuscripts of 1861-63*. It reads as follows:

> Productive labour—as value producing—always confronts capital as the labour of *isolated* workers, whatever social combinations those workers may enter into in the production process. Thus whereas capital represents the social productive power of labour towards the workers, productive labour always represents towards capital only the labour of the *isolated* worker.[63]

If by some miracle parliaments passed a law tomorrow, even unanimously, that from the day after tomorrow all this should be different—ie that the social power of productive labour should be recognised by capital and that productive labour should not be represented vis-à-vis capital as the labour of isolated workers—all that would not make the slightest difference. Nor could it. For capital, as materially constituted—through alienated and stored up labour—*actually* and *objectively* represents the social productive power of labour. This objective relationship of structural domination is what finds its adequate embodiment also in the political institutions of the capital system. This is why the plurality of capitals can be properly represented within the framework of parliamentary politics whereas labour cannot be. For the existing—incorrigibly iniquitous—material power relations make labour's "representation" either *vacuous* (as the *strictly political* parliamentary representation of the *materially subordinate* class of labour) or *self-contradictory* (whether we talk about the electoral representation of the *isolated* worker, or of the "democratic participation" of the radical *structural antagonist* of capital which is nonetheless happily predisposed to accepting the crumbs of marginal reform-oriented accommodation). No political reform can conceivably alter these material power relations within the parameters of the existing system.

What makes it worse for all those who are looking for significant change on the margins of the established political system is that the latter can claim for itself genuine constitutional legitimacy in its present mode of functioning, based on the historically constituted *inversion* of the actual state of affairs. For inasmuch as the capitalist is not only the "personification of capital" but functions also "as the personification of the *social* character of labour, of the *total workshop* as such",[64] the system can claim to represent the vitally necessary productive power of society vis-à-vis the individuals as the basis of their continued existence, incorporating the interest of all. In this way capital asserts itself not only as the *de facto* but also as the *de jure* power of society, in its capacity as the objectively given necessary condition of societal reproduction, and thereby as the constitutional foundation to its own political order. The fact that the constitutional legitimacy of capital is historically founded on the ruthless expropriation of the conditions of social metabolic reproduction—the means and material of labour—from the producers, and therefore capital's claimed "constitutionality" (like the origin of most constitutions) is unconstitutional, this unpalatable truth fades away in the mist of a remote past. The "*social productive powers* of labour, or *productive powers of social labour*, first develop historically with the specifically capitalist mode of production, hence appear as something immanent in the capital-relation and inseparable from it".[65] This is how capital's mode of social metabolic reproduction becomes *eternalised* and *legitimated* as a lawfully unchallengeable system. Legitimate contest is admissible only in relation to some minor aspects of the unalterable overall structure. The real state of affairs on the plane of socioeconomic reproduction—ie the actually exercised productive power of labour and its absolute necessity for securing capital's own reproduction—disappears from sight. Partly because of the ignorance of the very far from legitimable historical origin of capital's "primitive accumulation" and the concomitant, frequently violent, expropriation of property as the precondition of the system's present mode of functioning; and partly because of the mystifying nature of the established productive and distributive relations. For

the *objective conditions of labour* do not appear as subsumed under the worker; rather, he appears as subsumed
under them. CAPITAL EMPLOYS LABOUR. Even this relation
in its simplicity is a personification of things and a reification of persons.[66]

Nothing of this can be challenged and remedied within the
framework of parliamentary political reform. Nor even under
the most favourable circumstances, like the 1945 political land-
slide in favour of the Labour party, which followed in Britain the
revival of the critique of the system on account of the sacrifices
that had to be endured by the popular masses during the long
years of inter-war depression and the subsequent war. It would
be absurd to expect the abolition of the *"personification of things
and the reification of persons"* by political decree, and just as absurd
to expect the proclamation of such an intended reform within
the framework of capital's political institutions. For the capital
system cannot function without the perverse overturning of the
relationship between persons and things: capital's alienated and
reified powers which dominate the masses of people. Similarly, it
would be a miracle if the workers who confront capital in the
labour process as "isolated workers" could reacquire mastery
over the social productive powers of their labour by some political decree, or even by a whole series of parliamentary reforms
enacted under capital's order of social metabolic control. For in
these matters there is no way of avoiding the irreconcilable conflict over the material stakes of *"either/or"*.

Capital can neither abdicate its—usurped—social productive
powers in favour of labour, nor can it share them with labour.
For they constitute the overall controlling power of societal
reproduction in the form of *"the rule of wealth over society"*. Thus
it is impossible to escape in the domain of the fundamental
social metabolism the severe logic of *either/or*. For either
wealth, in the shape of capital, continues to rule over human
society, taking it to the brink of self-destruction, or the society
of associated producers learns to rule over alienated and reified
wealth, with productive powers arising from the self-determined social labour of its individual members.

Capital is the *extra-parliamentary force par excellence* which
cannot be politically constrained in its power of social metabolic

control. This is why the only mode of political representation compatible with capital's mode of functioning is one which *effectively denies* the possibility of contesting its *material power*. And precisely because capital is the extra-parliamentary force par excellence, it has nothing to fear from the reforms that can be enacted within its parliamentary political framework. Since the vital issue on which everything else hinges is that "the *objective conditions of labour* do not appear as subsumed under the worker" but, on the contrary, "he appears as subsumed under them", no meaningful change is feasible without addressing this issue both in a form of politics capable of matching capital's extra-parliamentary powers and modes of action, and in the domain of material reproduction. Thus the only challenge that could sustainably affect the power of capital is one which would simultaneously aim at assuming the system's key productive functions, and at acquiring control over the corresponding political decision making processes in all spheres, instead of being hopelessly constrained by the circular confinement of legitimate political action to parliamentary legislation.

To be sure, the castration of socialist politics is perfectly consistent with the power relations of capital and with its only feasible mode of operation, *in all its forms*. Since "the objective conditions of labour do not appear as subsumed under the worker", rather the opposite, therefore the worker treated as isolated worker in the labour process can be legitimately considered in the same way in the other important spheres of the societal reproduction and distribution process. In politics he or she can legitimately act as the (isolated) "electors" who make their decisions strictly alone in the privacy of the polling booth. And in the materially most important sphere of "productive consumption" which completes the cycle of capital's expanded reproduction, they can appear again as—strictly individual/isolated—"sovereign consumers" who bear no relationship to their class. Instead, they act by consulting—this time not their *"political and moral conscience"* in the secrecy of the electoral booth, as they did it in their capacity as "sovereign electors"— but their *"rational consciousness"* (or "rational faculty") in calculating and maximising their "private marginal utilities".

The Soviet type postcapitalist system retained the same relationship, despite the abolition of the private capitalist form of personification of capital. The worker remained subsumed under the objective conditions of labour, under the authoritarian control of the state as managed by the postcapitalist personifications of capital. Treated as isolated workers, who could under no circumstances organise themselves vis-à-vis the controlling authority of the labour process, they could be rewarded as "Stakhanovite" exemplary individuals (to be emulated by others), or punished and sent in their millions to the labour camps as "criminal saboteurs" and "enemy agents"; but labour as such could not acquire legitimacy as the active collective agent of the labour process, let alone assume control over social metabolic reproduction as a whole. Although under the prevailing circumstances of authoritarian "planning" the idea of "consumer sovereignty' could not be maintained, none the less the matter of consumption was also regulated on an individual—and at that as a rule most discriminatory—basis, both in relation to "Stakhanovites" and "exemplary party workers". Even the fiction of "secret ballots" was maintained, whereby the "socialist individuals" were supposed to consult their "moral and political conscience" in the privacy of the polling booth, and come up with the expected uniform state-legitimating answers. All this was by no means surprising. For substantive differences in the field of politics and in that of "productive consumption" would be feasible only by radically altering the structuring principle of the capital system which must keep the workers—one way or another—subsumed under the objective conditions of their own labour.

The extra-parliamentary power of capital can only be matched by labour's extra-parliamentary force and mode of action. This is all the more important in view of the complete disintegration of the once proclaimed and pursued parliamentary reformism of the labour movement, in the interest of delivering labour to capital as fragmented electoral fodder. Rosa Luxemburg wrote, prophetically, a very long time ago that:

> parliamentarism is the breeding place of all the opportunist tendencies now existing in the Western Social Democracy…[it] provides the soil for such illusions of current opportunism as overvaluation of social reforms, class and party collaboration, the hope of pacific development

toward socialism, etc... With the growth of the labour
movement, parliamentarism becomes a springboard for
political careerists. That is why so many ambitious failures from the bourgeoisie flock to the banners of the
socialist parties... [The aim is to] *dissolve* the active, class
conscious sector of the proletariat in the *amorphous mass
of an "electorate"*.[67]

The dissolution of which Rosa Luxemburg spoke as a threat
has been fully completed to date, using the notion of an
"amorphous electorate" as its ideological legitimatory
ground. Through this process not only openly reformist
Western social democracy but also the once programmatically
revolutionary affiliates of the Third International turned themselves into bourgeois liberal parties, consummating thereby
the capitulation of the "political arm" of labour before the
"rational" and "realistic" imperatives of capital. All this came
about much more easily than could be at first imagined. For
the process of dissolution and disintegration of labour's defensive strategies was objectively helped along and sustained by
the material power relations of the capital system which in the
process of production and consumption can recognise only the
isolated worker and consumer, and in the political domain the
isolated elector equivalent to the powerless worker. This is
why in the end "representational" politics had to be degraded
to the level of a public relations exercise everywhere, appropriately vomiting out of its belly and catapulting to the top of
parliamentary politics—instead of realising the promised
"Italian road to socialism"—"representative" creatures like
media tycoon Silvio Berlusconi,—of all places in the country of,
once upon a time, Gramsci's Communist party.

Naturally, in the countries of "advanced capitalism", against
the background of the clamorous historical failure of
reformism and representational politics in general, the much
needed change is unthinkable without the radical reconstitution of the labour movement—in its integrality and on an
international scale—as an extra-parliamentary force. The self-
defeating division between the "political arm" and the
"industrial arm" of labour proves every day that such a division
is a hopeless historical anachronism. Not only in view of its

obvious failure in the political arena in the course of a whole century, but also because of its inability to embrace within its framework the countless millions of the *unemployed* "superfluous people", ejected from the labour process at an alarming rate by the dehumanising imperatives of "productive capital". The labour force still employed, defining its strategies as an organised political movement, cannot afford to disregard any longer the profound grievances—as well as the great potential force—of these countless millions. All the less because tomorrow the same fate is bound to afflict growing sections of today still employed labour. Given the slavishly facilitating role of politics in the service of capital's mode of social metabolic control—ideologically rationalised and justified under the labels of "increased productivity", "competitive advantage", "market discipline", "globalisation", "cost-efficiency", meeting the challenge of the "five little tigers', or whatever else—very little can be expected from the parliamentary institutions as they are articulated today. Only a radical intervention at the level of the established order's wastefully "economising" material reproductive processes can successfully redress the powerlessness of labour, provided that it can assert itself against the now prevailing most unfavourable odds through the concerted action of a mass extra-parliamentary movement. This is what puts the historical actuality of the socialist offensive into relief.

It must be emphasised again that, as mentioned in Section 1.1, the historical actuality of the socialist offensive—due to the exhaustion of the self-serving concessions which capital could make in the past to a defensively articulated labour movement—does not mean that the success is assured and its realisation is in our immediate vicinity. Being *"historical"* here indicates, on the one hand, that the necessity of instituting some fundamental changes in the orientation and organisation of the socialist movement has appeared on the historical agenda; and, on the other, that the process in question unfolds under the pressure of powerful historical determinations, pushing the social agency of labour in the direction of a sustained strategic offensive if it wants to realise not only its potentially all-embracing transformatory objectives but even its most limited ones. The road ahead is likely to be very hard, and certainly not one that can be side-stepped or altogether avoided.

The historical *mediations* required as viable steps towards the realisation of labour's alternative social metabolic order are inherent both in the pursued objective—a radical intervention not confined to the political sphere but directly challenging the material structures of the capital-relation itself which subsume labour under the alienated and reified objective conditions of its exercise, condemning the social subject of the production process to the utter powerlessness of isolated workers—and in the inescapably extra-parliamentary mode of action through which it can be progressively translated into reality. For by the very nature of this enterprise, to have any chance of success at all, already the *first steps* must confront and overcome—even if at first only in relatively limited contexts—the pernicious diremption of politics and economics which suits only capital's mode of social metabolic control, as the self-defeating separation of labour's "political arm" from its "industrial arm" proved it with painful conclusiveness in the last hundred years.

It must be also stressed that the materially effective practical negation of the dominant reproductive structures through extra-parliamentary organisation and action does not imply lawlessness or even an aprioristic rejection of parliament itself. Nonetheless, it involves an organisationally sustained challenge to the crippling constraints which the parliamentary "rules of the game" *one-sidedly* impose on labour as the antagonist of capital. Naturally, the question of legislation cannot be ignored or wished out of existence even in a genuinely socialist society of the future. What decides the issue is the relationship between the associated producers and the rules which they set themselves through appropriate forms of decision making. To be sure, Marx is right that in a developed socialist society many of the unavoidable regulatory requirements can find their solution through *customs* and *traditions* established by the autonomous decisions and spontaneous interrelations of the individuals living and working in a non-adversarial framework of society. Without that the supersession of politics as an alienated domain is inconceivable, making therefore also the "withering away of the state" unthinkable. But it is also clear that for the foreseeable future many of the overall regulatory requirements of society are bound to remain tied to formal legislative procedures. This is why the "parliamentary wisdom of deluding others as well as oneself", quoted in Section 1.3, must be considered "so much the worse" and not "so much the better".

Thus the role of labour's extra-parliamentary movement is twofold. On the one hand, it has to assert its strategic interests as a social metabolic alternative by confronting and forcefully negating in practical terms the structural determinations of the established order as manifest in the capital-relation and in the concomitant subordination of labour in the socioeconomic reproduction process, instead of helping to restabilise capital in crisis as it happened at important junctures of the reformist past. At the same time, on the other hand, the political power of capital which prevails in parliament needs to be and can be challenged through the pressure which extra-parliamentary forms of action can exercise on the legislative and executive, as witnessed by the impact of even the "single issue" anti-poll-tax movement which played a major role in the fall of Margaret Thatcher from the top of the political pyramid.

Without a strategically oriented and sustained extra-parliamentary challenge the parties alternating in government can continue to function as convenient reciprocal *alibis* for the structural failure of the established order towards labour, thereby effectively confining the role of the labour movement to its position as an inconvenient but *marginalisable afterthought* in capital's parliamentary system. Thus in relation to both the material reproductive and the political domain, the constitution of a strategically viable socialist extra-parliamentaty *mass* movement—in conjunction with the traditional forms of labour's, at present hopelessly derailed, political organisation, which badly need the *radicalising pressure and support* of such extra-parliamentary forces—is a vital precondition for countering with success the massive extra-parliamentary power of capital.

NOTES

1 *Beyond Capital* (Merlin Press, London, 1995), p729.

2 Philip Bassett, "Labour shows it means to do business with business", *The Times*, 7 April 1995. The quotation is taken from a speech Tony Blair made on the 1 April 2005.

3 *Beyond Capital*, p730.

4 Parliamentary votes are now considered a mere formality, if that. Vital issues are never even debated in parliament. They are simply imposed on it with cynical manipulation, as the "approval" of the Iraq war happened to be in Britain, under the false pretence that Saddam Hussein's "weapons of mass destruction were ready to be fired in 45 minutes", in prime minister Tony Blair's words. Moreover, it is well known that as a matter of routine the political decisions are not made even by the members of the Cabinet—who only rubber stamp them—but by less than a handful of people in the so called "kitchen cabinets". And all this is done in the name of democratic parliamentary politics.

5 Rosa Luxemburg, "Organisational Questions of the Russian Social Democracy", in the volume *The Russian Revolution and Leninism or Marxism* (University of Michigan Press, Ann Arbor, 1970), p98.

6 Rousseau, *The Social Contract* (Everyman edition), p78.

7 Rousseau, as above, p79.

8 Discussed in chapter 14 of *Beyond Capital*.

9 As above.

10 Adam Smith, *The Wealth of Nations*, edited by J. R. McCulloch, (Adam and Charles Black, Edinburgh, 1863), p200.

11 As above, p273.

12 Lenin made it amply clear that "*political* revolutions can under no circumstances whatsoever either obscure or weaken the slogan of a *socialist* revolution…which should not be regarded as a *single act*, but as a *period* of turbulent political and economic upheavals, the most intense class struggle, civil war, revolutions and counter-revolutions." Lenin, "On the Slogan for a United States of Europe", *Collected Works*, Vol. 21, p340.

  Whereas Lenin always retained his awareness of the fundamental difference between the political and the ongoing social revolution, even when he was irrevocably forced into defending the bare survival of the political revolution as such after the dying down of the revolutionary wave in Europe, Stalin obliterated this vital distinction, pretending that the unavoidable *first step* in the direction of the socialist transformation represented socialism itself, to be simply followed by stepping onto the "highest stage of Communism" in an encircled country.

13 As Marx puts it, in the course of so-called primitive accumulation capital emerges "dripping from head to foot, from every pore, with blood and dirt". See Part VIII of Marx's *Capital*, Vol. 1, "The So-called Primitive Accumulation".

14 Hegel, *The Philosophy of History* (Harper Torchbooks), p457.

15 Marx, *Economic Manuscripts of 1861-63*, in Marx and Engels *Collected Works*, Vol. 34, p457. Another important qualification that must be added here is that "Productive labour—as value producing—always confronts capital as the labour of *isolated* workers, whatever social combinations those workers may enter into in the production process. Thus, whereas capital represents the social productive power of labour towards the workers, productive labour always represents towards capital only the labour of the *isolated* worker." As above p460. Marx's emphases.

16 As above, p456.

17 As above, p457.

18 The points made in the last paragraphs are more fully discussed in Section 18.4 of *Beyond Capital*: "The Need to Counter Capital's Extra-parliamentary Force", pages 87-141 of the present volume.

19 *Beyond Capital*, p146.

20 Lenin, "On the Slogan for a United States of Europe", *Collected Works*, Vol. 21, pp339-40. (Written in August, 1915.)

21 Marx, *The Poverty of Philosophy* (Lawrence & Wishart, London, n.d.), p123.

22 Marx, *Lohn, Preis und Profit* (*Wages, Price and Profit*), Marx Engels Werke, Vol. 16, p153.

23 As above (Marx's italics).

24 "apart from the fact that this was merely the rising of a town under exceptional conditions, the majority of the Commune was in no sense socialist, nor could it be. With a small amount of sound common sense, however, they could have reached a compromise with Versailles useful to the whole mass of the people—the only thing that could be reached at the time." Marx, Letter to Domela Nieuwenhuis, 22 February, 1881.

25 As above.

26 "Speech Delivered at a Meeting of Activists of the Moscow Organization of the RCP(B), December 6, 1920". Lenin, *Collected Works*, Vol. 21, pp441-2.

27 Reporter's Record of the Speech Made by Marx at the Meeting Held in Amsterdam on September 8, 1872. (See MEW, Vol. 18, p160.)

28 Marx, Letter to NF Danielson, 19 February, 1881. (MEW, Vol. 35, p.157, Marx's italics.)

29 Marx, *Grundrisse*, p408, p410. (German edition: p311, pp313-4.)

30 As above, pp409-10. (German edition: p313.)

31 These problems have been discussed in Chapters 15 and 16 of *Beyond Capital*. The fact that the end of the cold war failed to deliver the "peace dividend", leaving the military / industrial complex in a dominant position in the leading capitalist countries, underlines the importance of these deep-seated economic connections.

32 *The Times*, 22 September, 1981.

33 Engels, Letter to A Bebel, 1-2 May, 1891.

34 Marx, Letter to Wilhelm Bracke, 5 May, 1875.

35 Lukács, "Tactics and Ethics" (1919), in *Political Writings, 1919-1929* (New Left Books, London, 1972), p31.

36 *The Sunday Times*, 21 February, 1982. We can see, again, how the desperate imperative of a blind submission to capital's economic determinism is used by decreeing the recognition of "no alternative" (yet another bourgeois "law of nature") as the unquestionable criterion of "sanity" and freedom.

37 It is highly misleading to represent these two as polar opposites, with

the suggestion that the latter introduces some major innovation in relation to the former. As a matter of fact, for a long time every variety of Keynesianism has been a Quixotic venture that carried *within itself* its Friedmannesque Sancho Panza—in the "stop" phase of its "stop-go" policies—and *vice versa*. But perhaps a more fitting way of grasping their true significance and impact is to recognise them as the cancer that they are in each other's bowels, reciprocally intensifying the consequences of their separate action. The fact that the cancer of monetarism had to surface recently in such a particularly obnoxious form from the Keynesian entrails— openly supporting with its claimed "enlightened" views the most brutal military dictatorships, from Chile to El Salvador, not to mention the all-powerful US military-industrial complex—only shows that the pretence of unproblematical (indeed: model) "development" can no longer be maintained. In the meantime, the momentum of an oscillatory swing in the other direction is slowly but certainly building up: no doubt, before long we are going to be presented with another variant of Keynesian miracle-making, even if for a much shorter duration than the "happy days" of postwar expansion. In this sense, as capital's apologists continue to remind us of the phrase, truly "there is no alternative". But to expect the restoration of capital's health to its former vigorous state by either of the two, or indeed by both put together, is—alongside the *fiat* of "sanity"—another striking example of the dangerous wishful thinking that dominates our social/economic life today.

38 "Imagine the government, in its wisdom, set up a panel of experts whose brief was to devise a system to give privatisation a bad name.

Step one would be to transfer monopoly utilities into the private sector with the minimum of competition and, for the first five years, a very generous pricing regime. Step two would be to appoint regulators who, having allowed these privatized utilities to build up a huge profits base, would lean towards the interests of shareholders rather than customers, in deciding the industry's pricing structure. Step three, a vital one this, would be to allow the directors and chairmen of these privatized utilities to confirm that monopoly industries deal in Monopoly money, by paying themselves huge salaries, with share options and golden handshakes. Never mind that many of these people do not have an entrepreneurial bone in their bodies. Never mind that most have never taken a risk in their lives. They seem to be motivated by the motto from the 1980 film *Wall Street*: 'Greed is good'. The government, then, has no need for such a panel. The existing system does the job very well."

If someone thinks that this quotation comes from a socialist fringe publication, they are in for a big surprise. For it is taken from an editorial article—under the title: "Privatization is now a dirty word"—which appeared on 14 August 1994 in by far the biggest circulation British conservative weekly paper, *The Sunday Times*. In fact the Editorial article concludes with a broken heart: "This newspaper supports privatization. We have no truck with those who criticise the financial rewards that accrue to those who display genuine enterprise. Sadly, the government has made it all too easy for the once good name of privatization to be dragged into disrepute."

39 "Burden of opposition", *The Times*, 11 August 1995.

40 Hegel, *The Philosophy of Right*, p201.

41 Robert Taylor, "Blow for unions in
    derecognition case", *Financial Times*,
    17 March 1995.
42 As above.
43 Attila József, Eszmélet
    ("Consciousness"). In József's
    words:

    ...ingyen keresek
    bizonyosabbat mint a kocka.
    Nem dörgölödzik sült lapocka
    számhoz s szivemhez kisgyerek—
    ügyeskedhet, nem fog a macska
    egyszerre kint s bent egeret.

    In rough translation the passage
    reads like this:

    ...I get nothing for trying to find
    something more secure than dice.
    No roast rib touches my mouth
    nor a small child my heart—
    even the best tricks of cat won't catch
    the mouse
    at the same time outside and inside the
    house.

44 Rousseau, *The Social Contract*
    (Everyman Edition), p.78.
45 As above, p79.
46 As above, p42.
47 Hugo Chávez Frias, *Pueblo, Sufragio*
    y Democracia (Ediciones MBR-200,
    Yara, 1993), pp5-6.
48 As above, p9.
49 As above, p11.
50 As above, pp8-11.
51 As above, p9.
52 See Norberto Bobbio, *Politica e*
    Cultura (Einaudi, Torino, 1955); *Da*
    Hobbes a Marx (Morano Editore,
    Napoli, 1965); *Saggi Sulla Scienza*
    Politica in Italia (Editori Laterza,
    Roma & Bari, 1971); *Quale*
    Socialismo? Discussione di
    un'alternativa (Einaudi, Torino,
    1976); *Dalla Struttura alla Funzione:*
    Nuovi Studi di Teoria del Diritto
    (Edizioni di Comunità, Milano,
    1977); *The Future of Democracy: A*
    Defence of the Rules of the Game
    (Polity Press, Oxford, 1987).
53 As Bobbio puts it:

    Today the priority is not only the
    right to freedom and the right to
    work and social security, but also to
    take an example the right of
    humanity today and of future
    generations to live in an unpolluted
    environment, the right to self-
    regulated procreation, the right to
    privacy against the State's capacity
    to know everything we doing. Let
    me point too to the serious threat
    posed by technical progress in
    biology, a threat that can only be
    countered by establishing new
    rights. [Editor's translation].

    See Norberto Bobbio, 'Nuevas
    fronteras de la izquierda', in
    Leviatán, No. 47, Madrid, 1992.
    Quoted in Gabriel Vargas Lozano,
    Más allá del Derrumbe: Socialismo y
    Democracia en la Crisis de Civilización
    Contemporánea (Siglo XXI Editores,
    México & Madrid, 1994), p117. See
    especially the chapters 'Opciones
    después del derrumbe' and 'El
    socialismo liberal' for the author's
    thoughtful comments on Bobbio's
    work.
54 Peter Kellner, 'Blair can reinvent
    socialism—if he finds the right
    words', *The Sunday Times*, 9 October
    1994.
55 'Harold Macmillan at 85: An
    Interview', *The Listener*, 8 February
    1979, p209.
56 James Dale Davidson is the founder
    and chairman of the right-wing
    National Taxpayers Union "and the
    driving force behind the
    Constitutional Convention to
    Balance the Budget", according to
    the blurb of his book quoted below.
    His success in balancing the US
    Budget may be a good measure also
    of the soundness of his theories.
57 James Dale Davidson and Sir (now
    Lord) William Rees-Mogg, *Blood in*
    the Streets: Investment Profits in a
    World Gone Mad (Sidgwick &
    Jackson, London 1988) pp156-7. The
    title of the book refers to Baron

Nathan Rothschild's celebrated dictum: "The time to buy is when blood is running in the streets."

58 As above, p157.

59 See Noam Chomsky, 'The Responsibility of Intellectuals', in *The Dissenting Academy*, edited by Theodore Roszak (Random House, New York, 1967, and Penguin Books, Harmondsworth, 1969).

60 Philip Bassett, 'Labour shows it means to do business with business', *The Times*, 7 April 1995. Tony Blair made his confession on heading the party of British business before Labour's women conference in Derby on the 1st of April 1995.

61 As above. Labour's recently launched "Commission on Public Policy and British Business", as we learn from Philip Bassett's *Times* article, "will include among a host of luminaries David Sainsbury, head of the supermarket group, [Yeltsin adviser] Professor Richard Layard of the London School of Economics, and Sir Christopher Harding, former chairman of British Nuclear Fuels and for 20 years a director of Hanson, one of the Conservative party's biggest donors and most active business supporters."

62 "President Mandela delivered an important boost to South Africa's expanding multimillion-pound arms industry yesterday by publicly giving it his personal blessing for the first time… His public endorsement was welcomed by South Africa's arms manufacturers, who believe his support will help them to secure future deals. Abba Omar, speaking for Armscor, the state arms agency, said: 'The President has for the first time unequivocally given his backing to the arms industry. It cannot be stressed how important his seal of approval is to us'." Inigo Gilmore, "Mandela applauds South Africa's rising arms trade", *The Times*, 23 November 1994.

63 Marx, Engels, *Collected Works*, Vol.34, p460. Marx's italics.

64 As above, p457. Marx's italics.

65 As above, p456. Marx's italics.

66 As above, p457. Marx's italics and upper case emphases.

67 Rosa Luxemburg, "Organizational Questions of the Russian Social Democracy", *or Marxism?*, p98.

GLOSSARY

Bernstein Eduard Bernstein (1850-1932), was a leading figure in the German Social Democratic party who in the 1890s argued that Marxism should be "revised" and revolution rejected.

"historic compromise" Proposal in the late 1970s by the Italian Communist party, then one of the biggest in Western Europe, for alliance with the dominant party of postwar Italian capitalism, the Christian Democrats. The claim was that this was necessary to defend democracy.

Harold Wilson Labour prime minister 1964-70 and again 1974-76.

Glasnost see Gorbachev, Mikhail

Gorbachev, Mikhail General Secretary of the Communist Party of the Soviet Union between 1985 and 1991, who initiated an attempt at reform in response to the deepening crisis of the Stalinist system. "Glasnost" (opening) aimed at allowing some popular pressure to be put on the ruling bureaucracy to allow "perestroika" (restructuring), effectively to allow an opening to market reform.

Ontological Term used in philosophy to refer to the intrinsic nature of existence or reality.

de jure In law.

"past Internationals" See First, Second, and Third International

"übergreifendes Moment" Predominant element.

First International International Working Men's Association, also known as the First International, grouped together socialists and trade unionists. It was founded in 1864 and formally dissolved in 1876. Karl Marx was a key figure.

Paris Commune 1871 uprising by workers and artisans in Paris that established a revolutionary government lasting 72 days before being brutally crushed.

Gotha programme Programme of the German Social Democratic party adopted at its foundation in 1875. Marx was critical of aspects of this, see his *Critique of the Gotha Programme*.

Second International Grouping of socialist parties formed in 1889. While most claimed adherence to Marxism, the majority supported their own ruling classes in the First World War.

German "March Action" Disastrous attempt by German Communist party to turn local conflict in mining region of Mansfeld into an insurrectionary movement, despite lack of support across the working class as a whole.

Yalta agreements Meeting between Stalin, Roosevelt and Churchill to agree on postwar division of the world.

Reculer pour mieux sauter To draw back in order to jump better.

Brandt Commissions International committee established in late 1970s to promote development in poor countries, headed by German Social Democrat Willie Brandt.

Edward Heath British Tory prime minister 1970-74.

Mr Haig Alexander Haig, US Secretary of State under Ronald Reagan.

Sino-Soviet conflict Conflict between China and Soviet Union that saw Mao's China increasingly assert its independence. Led to armed border clashes between the two states in 1969.

China–Vietnam war Bloody border clashes between China and Vietnam in 1979.

Bakunin Mikhail Bakunin (1814-1876) was an influential Russian anarchist.

a posteriori Here: after the fact.

John Stuart Mill and *negative freedom* Influential liberal philosopher (1806-1873). Negative freedom refers to freedom to act without interference or coercion by others.

Christian Democrats, Italy See Historic compromise

Japanese one-party system Post-war Japan was dominated by the Liberal Democratic party, though it was decisively beaten in the 2009 elections.

Helmut Schmidt Social Democratic Chancellor of West Germany 1974 to 1982.

apriori A proposition that said to be true, or false, without reference to experience; a self-evident truth (from Latin: "what comes before").

EEC European Economic Community; now the European Union (EU).

Stop-go **policies** Government economic intervention to alternatively boost demand to avoid recession, then curtail demand to avoid inflation and excessive imports. Associated with UK government policy in 1950s and '60s.

Friedmanesque After Milton Freidman, US economist and key ideologue in the return of free market ideas in 1970s.

Roy Hattersley Former deputy leader of the British Labour party.

Miners' strike Year long strike by British miners 1984-5 against Margaret Thatcher's Tory government's plans to shut pits. Ended in defeat.

Hugo Chavez Frias Better known now as Hugo Chavez. In 1992 Chavez led a failed military coup attempt against the regime that had violent repressed discontent in the late 1980s. Chavez was elected president of Venezuela in 1998 and is a proponent of a radical 'Bolivarian' revolution.

Rafael Caldera President of Venezuela 1969 to 1974 and again 1994.

Labour of Sisyphus In Greek myth Sisyphus is condemned to eternally push a boulder up a hill only to see it roll back down again.

Third International Initially the grouping of revolutionary socialist (Communist) parties that rallying to the Russian Revolution, braking with the reformism and chauvinism of the Second International. Later become an instrument of Stalinism.

Italian road to socialism The Italian Communist Party proclaimed this as its strategy, which was held to be neither the classic model of revolution along the lines of 1917 nor the social-democratic view of reform via parliamentary representation. In fact, it acted as cover for the adoption of the latter approach.

Mutatis mutandis From Latin and meaning: the necessary changes having been made.

Causa sui First cause, sometimes used by religious philosophers to refer to an argument for the existence of God (from the Latin: "cause of itself/himself").

Max Weber German theorist (1864-1920). Key figure in the emergence of sociology as a discipline. His ideas are often counter-posed to Marxism.

Sui generis Latin expression meaning of its own kind, or unique.

Butskellism Phrase expressing the political consensus between the main parties in British politics during he 1950s, taken from Rab Butler, the Conservative Chancellor and Hugh Gaitskell of the Labour party.

Harold Macmillan British Conservative prime minister 1957 to 1963.

Lib-labouring Alliance between Labour and Liberals.

New World Order In the wake of the end of the Cold War and collapse of the Soviet Union, then US president George Bush senior proclaimed a new era of peace and prosperity underpinned by US dominance.

Bellum omnium contra omnes War of all against all.

Ramsay McDonald Labour prime minister who broke with Labour party to form a coalition with the Tories in 1931.

Bettino Craxi Italian Socialist party prime minister 1983-87. Fled Italy in the wake of corruption investigations in the early 1990s.

Felipe Gonzales Spanish Socialist prime minister 1982-1996.

Francois Mitterrand French president 1981 to 1995, only Socialist party head of Fifth Republic.

Stakhanovite Named after the "exemplary" Soviet worker, Aleksei Stakhanov, who supposedly massively exceeded his production targets during the 1935 Five year plan.

Five little tigers Nickname for the industrialising economies of East Asia.

Anti-poll tax movement Mass movement against Margaret Thatcher's introduction of a highly inequitable local government tax in 1989-90, culminating in a riot in Trafalgar Square and helping drive Thatcher from office.

NAME INDEX